How Far Is It From Richmond To Heaven?

Thomas Higgins

WestBow
PRESS
A DIVISION OF THOMAS NELSON

WestBow Press books may be ordered through booksellers or by contacting:

WestBow Press
A Division of Thomas Nelson
1663 Liberty Drive
Bloomington, IN 47403
www.westbowpress.com
1-(866) 928-1240

Because of the dynamic nature of the Internet, any web addresses or links contained in this book may have changed since publication and may no longer be valid. The views expressed in this work are solely those of the author and do not necessarily reflect the views of the publisher, and the publisher hereby disclaims any responsibility for them.

Any people depicted in stock imagery provided by Thinkstock are models, and such images are being used for illustrative purposes only.

Certain stock imagery © Thinkstock.

ISBN: 978-1-4497-8246-7 (sc)

Library of Congress Control Number: 2013900975

Printed in the United States of America

WestBow Press rev. date: 1/28/2013

Table of Contents

The Journals

MY PURPOSE

There is a chronic need for finding homes for special needs persons whose families are aging, and the church and its members can make it happen. Churches support foreign missions where a small group of people go abroad or somewhere in the United States (at some cost), and do good things for others. Why not support a local ministry that will bring peace of mind to <u>local</u> families, and one in which all of the church members can have the satisfaction of being involved physically and financially in their own community.

Parents and caregivers realize that there are many families in our own neighborhoods with similar challenges. Families need to band together for a common cause. ARC, Community Services Boards, Knights of Columbus, Hope Tree Family Services in Virginia, and other organizations work together to make things happen.

Who are special needs people? What is the difference between Mental Retardation and Mental Illness? Are these special needs people able to work? Do they have a sense of humor? Do they have friends? If they are not normal shouldn't they live in state institutions? The public needs more exposure to these folks by getting to know them at church, in the community, and in the work place. I want everyone to know that these individuals can contribute to society and their community with loving guidance from caregivers.

Potential group home caregivers need to know how rewarding it can be. The job will not make them a financial fortune but can be so personally satisfying. The ideal employee does not have to be a college graduate. The best person for the job is simply someone with common sense and love in his or her heart for this population.

DEDICATION

This book is dedicated to God and Kathy West and her parents, Ken and Vivian West.

ACKNOWLEDGMENTS

To my wife Anne, who experiences the same love and satisfaction that I do in working with mentally disabled folks.

To Virginia Baptist Children's Home- Hope Tree Family Services (formerly called Developmental Disability Ministry -DDM), who partnered with Fredericksburg Baptist Church to build two Christian group homes in Fredericksburg, Virginia. They provided fourteen years of employment for Anne and me in a profession that came with much personal satisfaction.

To Fredericksburg Baptist Church for providing a Sunday School Ministry Class for over thirty years that is called "Special Friends." We appreciate their continuing loving support for the class and for the Mary Kelly and Howard Cates Group Homes.

To the Rappahannock Community Services Board for introducing me to the world of care giving. They invested in me through training seminars and on-the-job experiences. I worked with them full and part time, for a period of ten years.

To members of the Riverside Writers in Fredericksburg for suggestions and advice in the writing of this book.

To the parents and guardians who have shared their life experiences with me.

To my "Special Friends" who share their love, trust, and friendship with me.

FOREWARD

If thirty years ago I had been told that I would change occupations and begin working with mentally disabled folks after I reached the age of fifty-five, I would not have believed it. I had a degree in Business Administration from Virginia Tech. After completing college I worked as a Junior Industrial Engineer at a cellophane producing plant for seven years in Fredericksburg. I then did personnel work in Washington D.C. for the Department of Agriculture for another seven years. During that time my wife and I opened a gift and florist shop that we ran for twenty-five years in Fredericksburg. Now we would begin a fourth career together of care giving for special needs folks.

God opened up a whole new world for us. We came in contact with a population of people previously unknown to us that we now love, learn from, and consider our friends. As I look back, I can see how He was directing our lives by putting things and people in our path, and preparing us for the most rewarding careers of our life.

This book describes the wonderful experiences we have had with human beings who just happen to be mentally disabled. It also tells of a loving church who ultimately built two group homes for twelve special people.

The title of this book is a result of a conversation that took place when Anne and I were working a shift at the ladies Group Home. One evening at the dinner table the residents and staff were having a devotion and we got on the subject of death. It was interesting that each resident made a comment about it. Barbara asked us if her dad was going to die. I replied that sooner or later all of us would die and that her dad would go to heaven. Leigh mentioned that she had two white poodles that lived with her parents in Richmond. She said that one of the poodles had recently died, and that made her sad.

About three weeks later Barbara and Leigh were sitting on the couch and Barbara said, "Leigh, on Easter Sunday I want to go with you to Richmond and see your two white poodles."

Leigh immediately replied, "I told you before that one of the poodles died!"

With no hesitation at all Barbara asked the question, "How far is it from Richmond to Heaven?"

We have learned that our folks have a strong and simplistic faith and we can certainly learn from that.

CHAPTER 1

CHILDHOOD MEMORIES

My parents brought me into this world on June 8, 1935. We lived with my grandparents and great grandmother in Caroline County, Virginia for the first nine months of my life. We then moved to Fredericksburg and lived in the Ashby Apartments so that my dad could be closer to his job. I believe another reason for the move was to no longer be dependent on his family.

My memories of living in the apartment were of not having many toys, but of having five or six different size large cardboard boxes. We lived on a first floor apartment that opened up onto a large back porch. I would take the boxes on the porch and assemble them in such a way that I had a make-believe castle. I would crawl around in them and be entertained for hours. I also remember finding an abandoned kid's scooter with pump-up tires that my dad fixed. He could fix anything and I enjoyed using the scooter and showing it to my friends in the apartment complex.

Another memory was the day I went into a closet and discovered that my parents had a box of twenty-four of my favorite candy bars- Milky Ways! I don't remember if I ate any of them that day but I was in seventh heaven!

The apartment complex was next to a pants factory. I would crawl up in one of the windows, make use of my five year old social skills, and talk with the ladies who were busy at their sewing machines. I had curly blond hair and they said I was cute. Wow, what happened? No longer cute and much less hair!

I remember seeing a new home being built behind the apartment building. Curiously, I watched the workmen each day as it progressed. A friend of mine, who also lived in one of the apartments, would go with me to the house after the workmen had left. It was a two story brick home. We enjoyed going to the second floor, and would go out the window onto the front porch roof and take turns jumping off into the large pile of sand close by.

One day when the brick construction crew had left, my friend and I went out a back window of the second floor onto the scaffolding that had been recently constructed. I led the way and walked down to the end and started to look around the corner of the house. The board on which I was standing extended two or three feet beyond the support. Suddenly it began tilting and at that precise moment my mother, looking up from the back porch of the apartments, screamed at the top of her voice. It scared me enough to have the presence of mind to take my other foot and step back, which caused the board to go back in place. I came down in a hurry. My mother was mad and crying. At the time I thought she had over reacted.

Daddy, in spite of the depression, had managed to get a job at the new cellophane producing plant in 1929. He worked hard and was able to save and buy a small lot on Sunken Road in the city. He contracted to build a Cape Cod brick home. I remember the electrician wiring the house was in an automobile accident (he had been drinking) and broke his leg. Daddy was concerned about the delay but was reassured by the electrician that the work would still be done. He would come on the worksite on crutches and sit on a cinderblock and would give my dad step-by-step instructions on how to wire the whole house. Daddy learned a new trade and the house was finished on a timely basis.

When I was six years old we moved into our new home. I made new friends and walked to school every day. My folks were not active in church during those first years on Sunken Road. Frances Dickinson, a neighbor who lived four houses down on the block, was a member of Fredericksburg Baptist Church. She invited me to go with her family. I never felt pressure to go to church. She attended Sunday school and then returned home to pick up her mom and return in time for church services. Therefore I had the choice of going to Sunday school and then coming home, or staying for both services. A number of my friends attended there and a few years later I joined and was baptized. The church was large, but filled with friendly people.

When I was ten years old, my parents told me that I would soon be having a sister or brother. I was very excited about this, and for some reason thought it would be neat if my mother had twins. Each night before I went to bed I prayed to God to let my mother have twins. I never specified brothers or sisters. My parents tried to prepare me for the fact that my prayer might not be answered. There had been no history of twins in our families and the doctor said nothing to indicate otherwise. Tests were not available at that time to indicate multiple births or determine the sex of the child.

On October 11, 1946 my sister Jenifer was born. Approximately 6 minutes later my sister Judy came into the world! My parents were indeed surprised and so was the doctor. Not me! I knew it was going to happen. God answered my prayer! I remember making good money helping my overwhelmed mom take care of them. I was making $15 a week during the summer months. I think they considered me more of a dad figure, than a sibling. To this day I enjoy the special friendship I have with my twin sisters.

I look back now at the sequence of events that took place in my early life. The scaffolding incident, my introduction to a church that would have a special ministry years later, and God's answer to my special prayer- were all decisive moments in my young life. God was beginning to mold my character and prepare me for my life's work.

And God said: *"Tommy, I have seen you as a young child learn some of life's lessons, given you good health, a supportive family, and blessed you. I need you to do my work when you are mature and full of my love. Go and prepare for what I have in store for you."*

CHAPTER 2

MY INTRODUCTION TO MENTAL RETARDATION (MR)

The first time I recall being exposed to MR was in 1946. When I was in elementary school in the sixth grade, I had a classmate friend whose name was Bobby Pyle. His father had a doctorate and was a professor at Mary Washington College in Fredericksburg, and his wife was also well educated.

I knew that Bobby was a bright student who came by it naturally. He had a younger brother named Jonathan. Looking at him, I knew that something was wrong. He had trouble walking and his speech was limited.

A number of times Bobby invited me and other classmates to the small farm where he and his family lived. I remember his family treating Jonathan like any other kid. They were determined that he be as much like a normal child as possible. I recall his participating in a game once with us which involved shucking six dozen ears of corn, and anyone finding an ear with multicolored kernels received a prize. He found one and was all smiles.

I admired Bobby for allowing us to visit, particularly with his retarded brother at home. I lost track of the family, after they moved away. I remember hearing horrible descriptions used by people in the community to describe Jonathan's condition. "Mongolian Idiot" and "Mongoloid" were some of the words. I am sure that today's medical diagnosis would have been Down syndrome. That's a term I am sure everyone has heard and which certainly sounds more humane.

My next experience did not take place until 1956, when I was a junior at Virginia Tech. My parents had a summer cottage at Fairview Beach on the Potomac River. I had a summer job in Fredericksburg and commuted a short thirteen miles each day.

I enjoyed walking early in the morning before heading to work. Many mornings before seven, I would see a young boy playing alone in the water, under the watchful eye of his mother. I would never see them any other time during the week or weekends. His mom was isolating her son and herself from the real and cruel world that didn't understand mental retardation.

I enjoyed that summer at the beach. My family's cottage

had special meaning to me. The family living in the cottage next door had three girls and one boy. I started socializing with them. The family had a boat and we went water skiing. We played croquet, badminton, and Canasta. We were in each other's company for the entire summer. I found myself attracted to one of the girls named Anne. One evening, near the end of the summer, everyone except Anne came out to play badminton. I asked where she was and found out she had a date. That was a wakeup call, and the next week I asked her out. We played tennis on the city courts in Fredericksburg and went to dinner. Two years later she became my wife. I married the girl next door! We went to Fort Lauderdale for our honeymoon, driving in her 1953 baby blue Chevy convertible with a white vinyl top. I have digressed.

I remember reading in a Virginia Operations Manual the definition for Mental Retardation. *"Mental retardation" means substantial limitation in present functioning. It is characterized by significantly sub average intellectual functioning, existing concurrently...etc. etc.*

Wow, that's a definition to try to memorize and absorb.

Ask a family of a mentally retarded son or daughter their definition. You will see and hear a gamut of emotions and feelings. MR is disbelief, denial, anger with God, and disappointment. It is a realization that their son or daughter will never reach the potential they had hoped. They will need a lifetime of care.

Ask the sibling to describe his or her feelings about a MR brother or sister. This person will never be normal, and it is awkward inviting his or her friend home. The sister or brother gets most of the attention during that crucial time they are growing up. Seeing their parents being physically and emotionally strung out by the situation makes them sad. Many parents get divorced. It is a known fact that the divorce rate is higher in families like these. The siblings see themselves as needing to be caregivers to relieve some of the strain of their parents. The family can easily become dysfunctional.

When and if the normal siblings are able to leave home and start a life of their own, they will probably be asked later to help provide for the MR sibling. The entire family is affected by the situation. I have heard parents say that they hope they can outlive their child, because they are so much in fear their son or daughter will not receive the loving care that they had provided. Parents would prefer to not pass this responsibility on to their other children. They already feel guilty that they were unable to give as much attention and nurturing to all of their children.

Ask a mentally handicapped person their definition of mental retardation. They may not know the school book definitions, but they know they are different. They strive to be like other people. They want to work. They want to marry. They want to have children. They want to drive a car. They want to live on a farm with a spouse and to care for the animals as one young lady told me. They want to grow a garden. They just want to be "normal!" Above all they want to be liked, to have friends, and not have people staring at them.

My definition of MR became more clearly defined forty-seven years later when I started my fourth career. Anne and I accepted the position of residential managers of two MR group homes.

As residential managers we wanted to provide an atmosphere where the special needs person could live as independently as possible, with loving and supportive supervision. We wanted the parents and siblings to feel that they could let go a little, and try to enjoy their remaining lives, knowing that their loved one was receiving good care in a Christian home.

Our folks in the group home will always enjoy visiting and hearing from their families, but now they have their own home. Not a single one of them became homesick when they moved in. It was a natural thing to do, just as their siblings had moved away from the family. Some of the parents, however, had to make major adjustments. They had guilt feelings of abandoning their loved ones. Many times we would talk with parents on the phone and reassure them they had made the right decision.

They would see in a short time their child, now an adult, begin to blossom in this new environment.

As residential managers we also wanted to create a normal home situation where the residents could feel loved and safe. We wanted a place where they could express themselves, have new freedoms, experience life, and more independence. We wanted to support them in their work experiences, their spiritual experiences, their home living skills, and social skills. Most of all we wanted to treat them as adults.

We felt that we were a good match for this job for several reasons. We had love in our heart for this population, had our own family experiences of our kids growing up, some common sense, and maturity. We were both in our late fifties when we started this new career.

CHAPTER 3

BEGINNING THE SPECIAL FRIENDS MINISTRY

In December of 1957 I graduated from Virginia Tech. Anne and I were married the following May, and in July I started six months active duty in the Army. Basic training was at Fort Knox, Kentucky and the last four months at Fort Chafee, Arkansas. It was a fast six months and they succeeded in getting off the baby fat. When I arrived home some family members said I looked too skinny, yet I was pleased. Maintaining a good physical condition would not be easy. My Army Reserve obligation continued for the next five and one-half years in Fredericksburg.

Anne and I worked at the local cellophane plant. Anne was a secretary and I was a junior industrial engineer. We were able to save enough money for a down payment on a new home within four years. Living in a one bedroom apartment was good, until our son Jeff arrived six months before the home was completed. We were pleased to move into a home with three bedrooms and two bathrooms. Four years later our daughter Karen was born and able to have her own bedroom.

During this time we were active members of Fredericksburg Baptist Church. I also became Sunday School Superintendent. Margaret Ingram had invited her neighbors Ken and Vivian West to attend our Church. They had a son David and a daughter Kathy (to whom this book is dedicated). Kathy was mentally disabled. Realizing that this would restrict the parents from attending, Margaret, Vivian, and I went to a church business meeting and asked that we start a special class that would care for Kathy and others during the Sunday school hour. The Church voted in favor of this program and the class began in July 1979.

As superintendent, I was assigned the duty of finding a room for this new class and found the perfect space. It was next to the outside entrance leading to street parking and located near the restrooms. This would meet the needs of our new folks.

The room was used for storing of hospital equipment such as wheelchairs, crutches, and canes. Items were loaned to church members who needed them. I found another room slightly smaller that could be used, but the equipment committee resisted this suggestion for change. We ended up taking the problem to the Church Administrative Council. I was amazed we were comparing the needs of handicapped folks with needs for storage space. We did get the room, and this was the beginning of "Special Friends."

This incident which took place over thirty years ago, began a ministry that our Church has lovingly continued to nurture. Realizing a need, the Church started a building campaign in 1992 and now owns two first-class group homes that provide long term care for twelve special needs adults.

Anne and I had our lives changed after we accepted the position of residential managers for the Mary Louise Kelly and Howard Cates Group Homes. We held this assignment for fourteen years and then continued working part-time after retiring in 2006.

And God said: *"I want Fredericksburg Baptist Church and its caring members to provide the physical and spiritual needs for my special ones, and their families."*

CHAPTER 4

A CIRCLE OF PEARLS

INTRODUCTION – In another chapter in this book (A Family Bonded) I will talk about Ken and Vivian West and their special needs daughter. In addition to handling this monumental task at home with Kathy, Vivian became a legal guardian to one of the members of our Special Friends Sunday school class, Patty Burris.

I asked Vivian if she would describe her experiences in the undertaking for inclusion in this book. She agreed and also provided the title to this chapter.

Patty was the second member of the Special friends Sunday school class. I saw an older lady leading her down the sidewalk to our door. Patty was dressed up in a pink dress and, of course, beads. The lady escorting her was her grandmother.

In a panic, I ran to Margaret Ingram who played piano for the class and said, "There is a lady headed our way. We won't know what she likes to do or how to work with her. We had no warning that she was coming."

"Margaret replied, "Jesus will know what to do."

Patty was to touch the lives of each person who worked in Special Friends class, but also the church members. She was our "outreach coordinator" of sorts. She was very social and beads were her thing. She had to walk up to a person to check out their jewelry and to show off her own. She also carried a purse full of pictures and playing cards which she shared all around. She had poor vision and thick glasses. When she came close to someone, she was really close—so that she could see.

One Sunday her glasses were broken and a church member quietly took a coffee cup around to the adult Sunday School Classes and by the 11:00 church service, Patty had the money to fix her glasses.
Patty wanted to be baptized and our loving pastors and church family received her from the waters into the church. Special Friends teachers gave her a beautiful cross necklace to celebrate this great day.

She had been raised by her grandmother who was up in age when Patty came to us. She was a lady of great dignity and cared for Patty so beautifully. It is difficult to imagine how she had the strength to do it. After several years, the grandmother became ill and unable to care for her.
Patty began her journey into varied places to live. During

*this time, we were working towards starting a church owned group home for exactly this reason. Folks like Patty grow up and caregivers grow old and living situations are few and most are terrible. Her grandmother's dream was for her Patty to live in **our** group home… a dream that would never come true.*

Wherever Patty lived, she came to church. She would remind us that February 14ᵗʰ was coming and that was her birthday. She loved all holidays.

In one of Patty's placements she was trapped in the bathroom and sexually assaulted. Her grandmother was horror stricken. I went to the community service board, sick that it had happened to one of ours. Because she had no legal guardian, she was considered under the law to be a consenting adult.

I went to the grandmother and asked if she wanted me to become Patty's legal guardian and she gratefully agreed. Lawyers donated their time and I took guardianship. Patty went into a group home run by the community services board. As her guardian, I had input into her care. She went to a day program for older clients at the Rappahannock Adult Activity Center and life smoothed out for her. The grandmother was able to see these things before she passed away.

When you have a handicapped child in your family the number one fear that breaks your heart is: what if I die first and leave the child. Our church in its deep love for God and care for His children has put so many hearts to rest by giving a million times more than just a Sunday school class. They have met a lifetime of needs.

Patty's health began to fail and the decline was fast. She lived to the age of fifty-five. Her grandmother had somehow managed to save a small amount of money for Patty. When I became the legal guardian she asked me to take it. I was only guardian of her person and not her payee, but I took the money and kept it, securing it with two other signatures and my own.

Patty left us on December 4th. I took her aunt to the funeral home to arrange the final service. The grandmother had provided for the lot, vault, and insurance for the burial. The aunt told the funeral director that she did not have the money to open the grave. I said, "Oh yes, Grandmother has seen to that." I turned over the money entrusted to me. "Thank you, Grandmother!"

At Patty's funeral, the folks from her activity center released fifty-five pink balloons. A friend helped me make circles of strung pearls tied off with white ribbon. We took them in a basket and asked those at the grave side to put them on their Christmas tree in memory of Patty. We put them on the Christmas tree in the church sanctuary. I put them on the family tree every year and think of my friend, Patty Burris.

What a fitting tribute to a lady who loved beads. Surely God looks upon us, who love Him, as His "Circle of Pearls" surrounding His special children with loving care.
Vivian H. West

Before our church opened our group homes, I worked at the community service board group home where Patty lived in Spotsylvania County. When I learned of her death I wrote down some of my thoughts. I envisioned her journey into Heaven as being that of meeting God, showing him her beautiful beads and asking about Jesus and her Grandmother.

Whenever I worked with Patty she never failed to ask about my wife, Anne. I will miss her sweet waddling walk down the long hallway at the group home holding her beads, pocketbook, and playing cards wrapped with a rubber band.

And no one will forget the Easter Sunday morning when she walked into the class and declared, "He ain't dead!"

CHAPTER 5

A MESSAGE FROM GOD

The Special Friends Ministry began with one student and that, of course, was Kathy West. Her mom, Vivian, Margaret Ingram and Gail Hylton were the teachers. Gail, a special education teacher in the Stafford County Schools, told the parents and students about the class. New members were recruited. When the ministry began, Anne and I were enjoying being a part of a couples group, taught by Alice Hallberg. She was a creative and interesting teacher and we enjoyed the dialogue with her and the other married couples. We were all disappointed when she retired and decided to leave the area. Anne and I did not go to another Sunday school class. We became inactive, and for about two years were not going to Church at all.

Then I started going back on occasion, sitting up in the balcony, as I had done as a teenager. A few months later I "graduated" to the main sanctuary, sitting in the back center aisle. I equated this with sneaking back into church, hoping that God would not notice I had been goofing off.

Every Sunday that I went to church, I would see Special Friends Class members proudly walking up the aisle. Their ministry was expanding, and along with the three teachers were six or seven students. They took their reserved seats at the front left of the church, directly behind the Deaf Ministry section. I became a little emotional as they walked by me each Sunday. I was pleased to have been involved in helping them find a classroom several years before as Sunday school director, but I wasn't sure why these feelings surfaced now.

Then it happened. Waking up one morning it was spelled out for me very clearly. God spoke to me through a dream and immediately I knew that I needed to be involved with Special Friends. The very next Sunday I saw Gail Hylton in the church sanctuary, and told her I would like to help out. She invited me to come and join them. I did. Smiles and hugs greeted me. I instantly felt love and acceptance and wanted Anne to become involved with the class. Initially she resisted this idea.

One cold morning in January I woke up and had a gran mal seizure. Anne was scared to death. She heard me making noises as if I were choking and made the mistake of putting her hand in my mouth. I had a death grip but she finally managed to remove her hand and then called an ambulance to take me to the hospital. Anne went for treatment and a tetanus shot.

The cause for the seizure could not be determined, and it was thought this might be an isolated incident. However, thirty days later during a driving snow storm another seizure occurred before getting out of bed in the early morning. They had to get a second ambulance, as the first got stuck in the driveway. This visit to the hospital resulted in being put on medication.

The seizures never gave me any warning. I never knew they were happening, and particularly did not believe it when Anne told me it had happened a second time. I do recall that my chest was sore both times because of the physical contractions taking place during the seizure. Later, after ruling out some possible causes, my doctor believed that scar tissue had broken loose from the back of my head and could have triggered the events. Five years earlier I had fallen off a tall aluminum step ladder and landed on concrete. I was not unconscious but saw a few stars floating around.

I was told not to drive a car for one year. What a drag! Anne had to take me everywhere. We owned a gift shop and when she drove us to work she went up William Street each day, I was aware of a pothole in the middle of the road in one section, and it seemed like she hit it every day. I could not understand why she could not straddle it. On several occasions I reminded her to avoid it. One day she had reached her limit. She pulled the car over to the side of the road when she found a suitable place and said, "You can get out of the car and walk the last two miles or shut up!" I became quiet. Thank goodness they finally fixed the pothole.

Anne also drove me to Sunday school each week, went back home and returned for Church. I again suggested to her that she come join Special Friends Class so she would not have to drive so much. She said she did not feel comfortable with them, could not understand them when they spoke, and did not know what to say to them.

She finally agreed to come to the annual Christmas Pizza Party. When she met the members and felt the love, she too, was hooked and joined the class.

Today thirty people are on the rolls and on any given Sunday twenty or more members attend.

And God Said: *I am glad you got my message. I have plans for you and Anne that you would not believe, if I told you at this time in your lives.*

CHAPTER 6

ANNE'S INTRODUCTION TO SPECIAL FRIENDS

It is my belief that God in his infinite wisdom places us in life situations where we can learn and grow to be better disciples for him. Speaking just from my own personal life, God really had a challenge to move me in the direction he wanted. Some years ago I attended church but was not involved in a Sunday School Class. I was working in our gift and florist business six days a week, so I felt that I needed some time for myself. Some Sunday mornings after taking Tommy I came back home and took a nap. Tommy, however, had become involved in Special Friends Sunday School class so he would leave early and attend both Sunday school and Church services.

One December morning, Tommy had a gran mal seizure. He was admitted to the hospital, stayed overnight, and tests were run. He was told that in all probability he would never have another one and he could continue on his routine. However thirty days later he had another seizure. This time he volunteered to give up driving a car for a year and started medication. God was really testing me at this time. We had to change how we arranged our work schedule, and you know how it is to have a back seat driver with you all the time telling you to watch this bump or apply brakes for you when you really are in charge. Tommy needed to be at Sunday school, so I would drop him off, go back home and then return to Church. That didn't make a lot of sense. I became very frustrated and truthfully angry at times. Finally I decided that I would try attending a Christmas Pizza Party with Special Friends to see just what it was all about. I was very nervous and totally convinced that this experience would not be for me.

How wrong could I be? I came into the class room and received many warm hugs from the members of that class. I found if I could not understand what they were saying I could give a smile, and things were all right. We sang Christmas Carols, had pizza and a visit from Santa and a good time was had by all, especially me.
Needless to say on Sunday morning after that first initial visit, I became a part of Special Friends class and met many wonderful young men and women all very warm and loving and accepting of me, just as I was. God in his gentle loving way had given me a chance to know a whole new population of people and to change my future in many ways.

Chapter 7

EARLY CAREERS

After working at the local cellophane plant for seven years, I made a decision to look for another job. It was an easy decision, as I had been technically fired. They were just starting to lay off people and I was on that first "tidal wave" of employees to be terminated. Anne's office was not affected.

I was hurt and felt like a failure. My father took it harder than me. He had worked at this same plant since 1929 and although I did not know it at the time, went to my boss and chewed him out. The entire plant closed down several years later. My being fired was a blessing in disguise and my unemployment lasted only sixty days.

Bill Davis, a church friend of mine, worked for the Department of Agriculture in Washington D.C. and offered to take me to his personnel department of Rural Electrification Administration (REA). The agency was created by President Franklin Roosevelt in 1935, and its purpose was to provide low interest loans and expertise to electrical and telephone cooperatives serving undeveloped rural areas.

I accepted a job in the personnel department's Recruitment section, commuting from Fredericksburg each day. I enjoyed taking trips to Penn State and Virginia Tech, interviewing and recruiting engineers and accountants for the agency. I went to Fredericksburg Area Schools and administered secretarial tests and then made job offers, I liked this new job and the people working there. Anne continued working several more years as a secretary at the same plant that I had left.

Shortly after we married, Anne joined the Kenmore Garden Club. She was very competitive and had an eye for color. She enjoyed creating floral arrangements that she would take to club meetings for judging. Many a time I would come home from work and was banned from the refrigerator. She would take a shelf or two out and place the live arrangement in for conditioning until she left for the meeting.

Four years later we had started our family, and Anne was no longer working. She wanted to make some extra money and began buying materials from an artificial flower wholesaler in Richmond to make door wreaths. We anticipated running classified ads in the paper and having people come to our home to see and hopefully buy from the display in the basement. After discussing the feasibility of making any money this way, we came up with another idea.

Anne's high school friends, Donald and Louise Sparks owned a Laundromat in a local shopping center. We went to them and asked about renting a portion of the front window section, and they agreed. The space had a sixteen foot wide wall that went from floor to ceiling and sat back about three feet from the front display window. It shielded from view a laundry soap dispensing supply machine, a drink machine, and a juke box.

We agreed to pay a small percentage of everything we sold as rent. This was a good deal as we now had exposure to the public in a thriving shopping center. We improved the looks of the wall by stapling up green poly foil. The Christmas season was near, so Anne prepared eight different style Christmas door wreaths. We had extras packed away in barrels in the back room. Assorted color bows were made up and the customer had a choice of any wreath and bow combination.

I felt that we had a potential gold mine. The Laundromat employees would sell an occasional wreath during the day. They were paid fifty-cents for each wreath they sold out of the window display. I worked there in the evenings and all day Saturday.

I could not believe how good business was that first year. We almost sold out of everything. One evening, being very excited, I called Anne and told her we needed to order more materials from the wholesaler. She did not agree, and said she was content to sell out of everything before Christmas.

My cash register was my billfold. This particular night it appeared two inches thick with all of the bills (mostly ones) in my pocket. After getting home, I took the money and spread it on the dining room table in a semi-circle. Anne smiled, and was convinced to reorder supplies the next day. This was the beginning of a gift and flower shop named "Wee Wreath."

After that first year we branched out into flower arrangements and gifts. We were able to rent out a larger area in the Laundromat and paid substantially more rent. The next Christmas season we prepared for our first Christmas Open House. The laundry closed on Sunday at six p.m. We reopened at seven p.m. with Christmas wreaths on the wall display and a Christmas arrangement on the top of every washing machine. Several hundred customers attended. This Open House tradition continued for twenty-five years.

Anne was very creative and became busy enough to need additional part time employees. They brought even more talent to the business. After a few years we moved to another shopping center and opened up our own 1500 square ft. store. Anne started teaching flower arranging classes that increased traffic into the shop.

She would sometimes take the kids to the shop when she worked. They grew up in the business and occasionally we took them on our summer buying trips to Atlanta and New York. We had a great time and they were exposed to "The Big Apple." One of our ribbon suppliers would provide free tickets to a Broadway play. We also "allowed" our kids the opportunity to work in the shop with us where they learned good work ethics, which I believe is reflected in their job successes they each enjoy today.

Stocking the shop with gifts and supplies that we believed would sell was enjoyable, but it was not much fun in having to pay the bills when the shipments arrived. In the early days, I never would have imagined that I would eventually quit my good paying job in Washington. I did, and we opened up a second store in Ashland, Virginia. We gradually expanded our Fredericksburg business into a 4500 square foot florist and gift shop and remained in business for 25 years.

The business provided a fairly good living and we were able to send both of our kids to college. However in time our retail sales declined, and we felt God was closing a door. Changes would be coming.

CHAPTER 8

THE GROUP HOME PROJECT

Working with Fredericksburg Baptist Church Special Friends Ministry has been and still is rewarding. My wife and I have gotten very close to the other staff and the students. There is a warmth and love that is indescribable. When you walk through the door on Sunday morning you are welcomed with genuine smiles, hugs, and greetings.

As teachers we became aware of certain things. We were trying to fill our student's spiritual needs by doing simple object lessons, role playing, and singing. In the year 2000 color-coded musical bells were introduced to our ministry.

Eventually we learned more about their home situations. As the parents or guardians grew older, they became concerned about the care of their adult son or daughter. What would happen to them when the families could no longer provide the care needed?

One day a young lady came into our shop with her father. Her name was Annie, and it was apparent she was mentally handicapped. She was a small person and cast her eyes to the floor. When her father came up to the counter to pay for a basket, I mustered up the courage to mention to him that we had a Sunday school class that I thought she might enjoy. He said I should talk to her mother, and gave me the phone number before they left. A few days later I spoke with her mom, and we set up a Sunday morning for them to visit.

When that Sunday arrived, Annie and her mom walked into the room. She spent the entire Sunday school hour hiding her face in her mom's lap. The next Sunday her mom convinced her to stay in our class while she remained in her car on the street right outside. Annie stayed but kept her head buried in my wife's arms the entire time.

Things gradually got better and we realized this young lady had a complete vocabulary. She became one of our "helpers" and assisted us in doing crafts and setting up the classrooms. I attended her high school graduation party and took a small gift. I received a nice thank-you letter which I still have. A short time later her parents divorced. Her dad left the area and her mom became very distraught and concerned about Annie's future. Serious financial worries were a real concern for her mom.

We had a dream. Why couldn't we build a group home where Annie and some of our folks could live? I went to a church staff meeting and shared with them about some of our ideas:

1. We wanted our church to know more about the Ministry.
2. We shared with them some personal stories about some of our students.
3. As our membership was increasing, we needed to recruit more teachers and volunteers to help in the class.
4. We wanted to start a fund that could be used to build a home. This was to eventually be called the Special Friends Group Home Project.

The church administrative staff gave me permission to go to each adult Sunday school class and present the four-part plan. The first class I mustered up courage to visit was the Caverlee Class (named after the wife of a beloved former pastor who had presided over our wedding). Louise Jenkins was the class president and welcomed me with open arms. I was nervous, but realized that they were very receptive to what was being said. I distributed the handout and discussed the plan. They were among our strongest supporters through the years. All of the classes I visited were receptive to our planned project.

Soon members of our church started contributing money to the project as a means to honor someone's birthday, or as a memorial for a person who had passed. My wife and I had a friend named Ardi Hanson, who was a tole painting artist. When she had pattern books published, she tithed from the royalties she received. Over a period of about four years she contributed about $4000 to our project.

My parents also donated a few thousand dollars for several years. Our Church members and friends had contributed over $60,000. Annie's mom became a major contributor because a college classmate died and bequeathed in her will a substantial amount of money for the two of them.

Our committee, composed of our Sunday school teachers, became anxious to start a group home. I was ready for it to happen. My next door neighbor had a home for rent and was willing to make changes to meet our needs. However, we were not yet ready to make that bold a move. I believed it was time to do something and felt some frustration. We knew we wanted a first-class home that would provide good quality long term care where Annie and others could live, until such time they might need the services of a nursing home. We would need more than $60,000 to make this a reality.

A committee member, Margaret Ingram said it would come in God's time. I feared that it might not come in *my* time. There is still a need for more than 150 individuals to be in group homes in the Fredericksburg area. Some of these are critical because the parents are in nursing homes or have passed away.

And God said, *"Be patient my friends and you will see what I have in store for you and Fredericksburg Baptist Church."*

CHAPTER 9

DREAMS REALIZED

One day our Associate Pastor, Mike King, came to our committee meeting and said there was an anonymous benefactor willing to donate some property on Salem Church Road to build a group home. What a flash of good news that was! The donor of the property remained anonymous for several months. I wanted the whole community to know who this person was, because it was just the beginning of a miracle taking place at Fredericksburg Baptist Church. John and Barbara Mullins, and their son David and daughter-in-law, Shirley, were the benefactors. They are owners and managers of Covenant Funeral Service of Fredericksburg. This family is well loved and respected in the community.

A few months went by and a decision was made to organize an official Group Home Committee, composed of our original members, but now also others from the Church: Bill Young (a bank president), J. V. Kendall (a building contractor), and Bill Tignor (Social Services

Director of nearby Stafford County). Bill Tignor became our chairman. Dennis Sacrey, our Church Administrator, would be instrumental in handling financial matters as we progressed.

We started doing some serious planning, and felt we were on our way. At this point Larry Haun, our Pastor became actively involved. He told the Church he wanted to build this home. He began hearing from church members who were willing to donate professional services, money, and personal time to make the ministry a reality.

From time to time we, like other churches, had sent groups of church members to foreign lands to help others in need. Now we had begun a local ministry project in which every member of our church could be involved. I was impressed.

The committee was making some major decisions such as who would run the home. We contacted the local Rappahannock Community Services Board (RACSB) and had them attend some of our meetings. They already had the experience of opening one group home in Fredericksburg.

We also heard about a new ministry started by the Virginia Baptist Children's Home and Family Services located in Salem, Virginia. They had created the Developmental Disabilities Ministry (DDM). A Christian group home was just opening on the Salem Campus. Betty Burris, the Director of DDM, and Don Bradley, the Director of Virginia Baptist Children's Home, came and spoke with us. After much prayer and discussion, the committee decided that we should become a part of the DDM.

Our dreams became a reality in June of 1993 when Annie and five other ladies moved into the Mary Louise Kelly Home. My wife, Anne, and I were hired by Virginia Baptist-DDM and began working as Residential Managers.

Pastor Larry Haun and Associate Pastor Patti English took much pride in this church wide project. Patti had meaningful input in the interior decorating. We received a grant for $75,000 from the Catholic Organization, Knights of Columbus, to provide furniture and carpeting in the home. Our two pastors were visiting the property almost daily. The cost of construction was $150,000 and was paid for in the first year by the generous and loving congregation of our church. The home consisted of seven bedrooms, an office, kitchen, and a large living and dining room with cathedral ceilings. It also had four bathrooms, two of them large enough to accommodate three people at a time. We had a first class home. Today this home is probably appraised at over $400,000. God was making it happen.

John Mullins had a continuing interest in the construction of the home, and heard from Pastor Larry that we were getting ready to frame the home with sideboard to keep the cost down. John said that would not work, and wrote a check to cover the cost of bricking the entire home. He also paid for a brick patio built behind the home. J.V. Kendall, as contractor, donated hours of work at no charge.

I remember Pastor Larry later talking about his secretary, Audrey Ferrell. Someone suggested that the church provide inexpensive dinnerware for the group home. Audrey said she wanted to buy the best dinnerware and she and her husband, Bill, wrote a check for it. The china is still being used today and is in good condition.

There were many other instances of members giving sacrificially and it was a beautiful time in our church. The home was named after Mary Louise Kelly, our Church Organist and Minister of Children, a strong supporter of our Special Friends class. She died unexpectedly after surgery. Her family donated a piano to the home in her memory.

John and David Mullins came back to the church and offered to give us a rambler style brick home that was not being used, located next to the Mary Kelly Group Home. It was completely remodeled and furnished with new fixtures, appliances, and furniture. This was made possible by our church members and another contribution of $40,000 from the Catholic organization, Knights of Columbus. Pastors Larry and Patti once again were very much involved.

I remember one day seeing Larry climbing up a ladder and going on top of the roof checking on something. He was in his business suit and talking on his cell phone to someone. What a picture- our pastor preaching from the rooftop!

The second home would be for men. The Mullins family had known Herbie Embrey for a number of years. Herbie was a member of our church and Special Friends Sunday school class. He was well known in the church and community. He worked at Shoney's Restaurant washing dishes, bussing tables, and speaking to everyone who came into the restaurant. He also dressed up as the Shoney Bear Mascot from time to time. Herbie had a profound influence on our ministry. He was one of the first residents to move into the men's home.

In 1994 the Howard Cates Group Home opened and five men moved into their new home. It was named for our pastor emeritus, Howard Cates. Three years later Marrs Ferrell's family came to the Church and offered both money and property for a group home in which Marrs (blind since birth) could live. Our supervisor, Betty Burris, and our church made the decision to add on to the men's home.

A deck was removed from the back of the home and in its place an addition was built that included a cathedral ceiling living room, two bedrooms and a handicapped bathroom.

Fredericksburg Baptist Church owns and maintains both of these homes, and continues to love and support the residents and staff. Every year the deacons come and provide an ice cream social. Five or more of the Sunday school classes and church organizations bring covered dish dinners.

On August 2, 1993 two months after the opening of the ladies home, I realized that Annie (our first resident to move in the home) had indeed made much progress, and had a whole new life ahead of her. That was the evening that Margaret Garnett's Sunday school class brought a covered dish dinner to the group home. Approximately twenty-four people arrived to eat with all of us. After dinner Fred and Joyce, the other residential counselors, conducted a devotion for everyone. I thanked the class for helping to make this beautiful group home a reality.

Annie, who was sitting next to me, stood up and said she wanted to talk, announcing "I just moved into the group home and I am adjusting to living away from home. I love my house parents and want to hug them." She then came to me and the other counselors and hugged each of us. This shy young lady, who came to my shop five years earlier, stood up and told twenty-four strangers how she felt. That's progress.

These occasions continue to provide a wonderful opportunity for our residents to use their social skills, and to enjoy having fellowship with church members. In return our guests are able to get past the disability, and see people who are human, ambitious, humorous, and loving.

And God said: *"Unless the Lord blesses this house its builders labor in vain- Psalm 127-1"*

Mary Kelly Group Home

The Ladies of the Mary Kelly Group Home

Howard Cates Group Home

The Men of the Howard Cates Group Home

CHAPTER 10

SUPERVISOR, MENTOR, AND FRIEND

Iam convinced that God put Betty Burris in the path of Fredericksburg Baptist Church. She would do so much in guiding the direction we would be taking in starting our Christian group homes.

Betty was born and raised in Durham, North Carolina. Her parents were committed Christians and involved in helping people in their community. She was always an outgoing person even as a child. She had many interests and did well in elementary and high school.

She enjoyed visiting with her maternal and paternal grandparents who lived in other areas of the state. One grandmother "adopted" a family that had three children. One of these children had Down syndrome, although that term was not known at that time. The family was very protective of him. He was often isolated and Betty knew that he looked different but she wondered why the community and church did not include him in activities.

Because her grandparents had this family visit often in their home, Betty was allowed to play and be around him. He was shy with most people but once he knew you he would interact. He was hard to understand when he talked, and he was overweight. He was eating all the time, that being his comfort. He lived on the farm with his family and was isolated from the real world.

Betty attended Pfeiffer College and had a double major in Sociology and Christian Education. She did a field placement at a community center in Charlotte and worked with handicapped teenagers. She was intrigued by their abilities, and what they were capable of doing. She did some tutoring and was impressed with the positive changes she saw. At this time she began to think that she might like to work with persons with disabilities.

While in college she participated in a mission trip to Korea and other countries along the way. She witnessed cultural shock, which strengthened her desire to help people. Before she left she met her future husband Gene Burris who was going to seminary. As soon as she got back, he wanted to marry. They waited until her senior year.

Gene pastored a little country church and later a larger one in Raleigh. Betty realized that if she married a minister it would change some of her plans. In those days a pastor's wife working outside of the church was frowned upon.

She decided she would be a good pastor's wife but would not necessarily go with the flow. In other words she needed to do what was good for the church but would ultimately work with people with handicaps.

As Gene moved to pastor other churches, Betty became involved in a Special education program in a school close by. The school system paid her to return to college and get Special Ed classes. She started a Special Ed Program in two different elementary schools. This was an eye opener, as she studied abnormalities in children and their development. Whenever Gene relocated , Betty was able to start other programs in that community to help the handicapped.

After moving to Emporia, Virginia, Betty started a day support program requested by the Community Services Board (CSB). This helped handicapped individuals who stayed at home. At this time the school systems were not addressing the problem.

In addition to the day support program she also established a childhood education program. The program grew and included a workshop, an activity program, and support for family members, early childhood program, and helping people get jobs. All of this was done from one location, as it was a new concept. She worked with the local CSB to start a new group home.

They then relocated to Roanoke and worked with the local

Kiwanis Club to start a program for handicapped senior adults. With every move they made she felt God was placing her in places of need as she advanced her career. She then joined the Virginia Baptist Children's Homes in Salem, Virginia who were beginning a Developmental Disability Program (DDM). Their goal was to provide as normal a life as possible for special needs people, by providing programs and community housing for small groups and getting away from the institution concept.

She wanted to give families as much control as possible over their loved ones and to help them move from being caregivers to being just a mother, father, brother or sister to the handicapped person. This person would learn to become more independent in a loving and Christian atmosphere. This was a way for the Baptist churches in Virginia to get involved.

Our Church in Fredericksburg was one of the first to start a special needs Sunday school class. When she was invited to come and talk with our building committee, we knew she was talking our philosophy. It seemed only natural that our church in building the group homes would want to partner with their DDM program.

Betty said, "I remember the first time that a resident played the piano at your church. She was giving back to the community. That is one of the positive things that the group homes have done. Residents can feel good about sharing with other people and not feel ashamed.

What they do is quality and meaningful. Fredericksburg Baptist was the first partnership we had."

She believed that the group homes should house four to six residents with adequate staff to help them become the person they could become. They needed leadership and advice and loving assistance to help them become more independent. They should be involved in the community, have a job and be a part of the church. They should continue to have family connection. She, as supervisor, always encouraged us as staff to invite families for social events in the group home such as dinner invitations, resident's birthday and Christmas parties and picnics.

She encouraged staffing needs to be family oriented. Married couples, who were willing to be mentors and live with the residents, were a good model for the running of a Christian group home. Staff would help them make decisions about buying groceries, picking out their clothes etc. and would guide them through the learning process in a family like setting. Residents would understand that the group home employees were not parents, but people who lived with them, loved them, and were their friend.

It was a pleasure for Anne and me to have a supervisor and mentor who respected the concepts and ideas that we and our church envisioned. She allowed us to use our judgment in making many decisions, which made our job so very rewarding.

When she visited the group homes, she usually spent the night. We would spend hours exchanging ideas and talking into the wee hours of the night. She was our boss and we learned much from her.

Best of all, she was and remains our friend.

CHAPTER 11

MARRS FERRELL

Isaw Marrs in Church almost every Sunday. He sat in the middle section seats, adjacent to our Special Friends Class. I saw he was neatly dressed and usually sat with the same people, whom I assumed were family. His head was always bowed and eyes closed. I asked myself, "Can he talk? Is he mentally handicapped?" I learned later that he was blind since birth and forty-five years old. Little did I realize that he would become an important part of my everyday life.

I learned that his family members had approached our church and offered property and money to build a group home in which he could live. My supervisor, Betty Burris and Fredericksburg Baptist Church decided to expand the existing men's group home, rather than build another home. Betty and I made a visit in the home where he lived with his aunt. He had been reared in Texas and moved to Virginia to be with family when his mother died. His father had passed away some years before. He was very courteous and quiet-spoken. In the living room was a very nice Hammond organ that had come with him from Texas.

We had been told that he was musically inclined and asked him if he would play the organ for us. He walked over to the organ, extending his arms to protectively guide himself. When his foot hit up against the bench, he felt his way and sat down. He removed his shoes and moved over to the middle of the bench. He turned on the organ and played several recognizable tunes. I could not believe what I was hearing. Here was a mentally challenged blind man playing a two keyboard organ and using his stocking feet on the foot pedals below. One of the songs he played was a favorite of his aunt- "Are You Sincere?" This was a song recorded by Andy Williams, one of my favorite singers and I learned later, one of his.

I asked him if he liked to sing. He then, in a beautiful bass voice, sang "Sixteen Tons." He had perfect timing and inflections that sounded just like the rendition done by Tennessee Ernie Ford. I thought what a talent God has given this young man.

Several months later Marrs moved into the Howard Cates Group Home. I was getting him ready for bed that first evening and told him how glad we were that he was living at the Group Home. We told each other good night, and I started walking out of the bedroom.

He said something I did not understand, and I started to ask him what he had just said. Then I realized that he was reciting, "The Lord's Prayer". I felt like I was eavesdropping, but could not leave. He then prayed for his mom and dad and other family members. He then finished the prayer with, "Lord, thank you for letting me live with Tommy and Anne." I will not forget that evening.

I started talking with our Minister of Music, Mike Patch, to arrange a time that our Church could hear his beautiful voice. On several Wednesday nights we met with Tom Mulcahy, a choir member, who took an interest in our endeavor. We were thinking that they could sing a duet in church. Tom soon realized that Marrs held back his voice when they sang together. We then worked on him singing a solo. I attempted to feebly play the piano for several practices while Marrs sang "The Lord's Prayer" and "Amazing Grace". We found that he did not know all of the words to "Amazing Grace" but did a great job on "The Lord's Prayer." We knew this was the song for him.

The Special Friends Sunday school class was celebrating its 20th anniversary in July. Special recognition was to be made to a Boy Scout, Jimmy McGhee, who refurbished two of our classrooms for an Eagle Scout project. This seemed like a good time for Marrs to make his singing debut. On the Wednesday before this event, I took him to church to practice with the church organist, Shirley

Onderdonk. Mike turned on the sound system so Marrs would know what to expect. He sang it twice, beautifully. Shirley said that she thought he would do a good job on Sunday. I knew he would.

That Sunday came and I found myself a little nervous, but I did not let Marrs know. At the early service I led him up to the pulpit, helped him place his hands on the lectern for stability, and handed him the microphone. I introduced him by telling the congregation that he was a member of Special Friends Sunday school class, had just moved in to the Cates Group Home in December, and that God had given him an amazing voice.

The organ and piano began the introduction and the beautiful bass voice began. I got cold chills as he started singing and glanced at Church Staff directly in front of me, and discreetly looked at some of the audience. Many were wiping away tears. After the last note, there was applause. I floated off the stage guiding him back to his seat.

At the eleven o'clock service, when he finished singing, an even stronger applause took place. He was aware of it, and started applauding himself. After the church service a number of people came up to congratulate him. I was pleased that he had done such a good job and all of the church had heard him. To this day, I am moved every time he sings The Lord's Prayer in churches or civic groups. It is wonderful to see the audience reaction. I want the whole world to know about all of the Marrs Ferrells' who were put here on earth for a purpose!

I look back now after being retired and remember some special and fun times with him. One day after church I complimented him on his singing during the church service, because he was singing harmony during the closing hymn. His reply was, "Tom I have perfect pitch."

Another morning we had gone to Sunday school, and as usual, he and I went to the restroom before going to Church. He referred to it as "draining your radiator." One of the restrooms was busy with a number of people, so I led him to another small restroom in the building. I guided him into the stall. When he had finished I led him out to wash his hands. I then asked him to wait while I went in to "drain my radiator." In a few seconds he said to me in his bass voice, "I don't hear anything yet." I was becoming hysterical and having some difficulty performing the task. Then in a higher pitched voice I heard, "I still don't hear anything." It seemed as if it took me ten minutes to recover and get out of the restroom.

Marrs attends a nursing home day program during the week. He calls it the "Country Club," enjoys going there, and the food is good. He does crafts and always enjoys stirring up anything that is being made such as a cake or brownies. He is home on Mondays so I have been mentoring him for five hours each week. We have become buddies and do fun things.

As time goes by I find that he, and other special needs folks, is more comfortable with structured routine. We start with a twenty minute walk around the asphalt circular path located between the two group homes. We then run errands like taking trash to the dump or going to the bank. Before going to lunch we come to my home and he helps Anne mix the brownies. We then head for Burger King for a veggie burger, French fries, and ice tea (which he likes to stir, of course). Our next venture is to Giant Food where he helps me shop by pushing the grocery cart. I have to hold him back from trying to drive too fast down the aisles. Although I may need only a few items, we usually walk down all of the aisles so that we sneak in some more exercise.

We return to my home and sample the baked brownies and listen to Andy Williams and Frank Sinatra music for about an hour. When it is time to go he reminds me to give him the brownies to take back to the group home to share with his housemates. One day when returning home I told him: "Marrs I enjoyed being with you today."

His reply was: "Tom, you don't know how much I enjoyed being with you. Any time you need any help just call me."

Our friendship continues to grow. Since working with him I have learned more about blindness. He has never seen a blue sky, green trees, or a red rose. These are things we take for granted. He, however, has learned to compensate by keenly developing his other senses. A number of times when we are walking outside he will say, "The sun is beaming." Then I realize that indeed the sun is warm and shining on our faces. Another time he said, "Listen to the blue-jay." I had not been aware of the bird singing until he brought it to my attention.

We both enjoy music and one day while returning to the group home we were listening to Kenny Rogers singing a love song. Marrs said to me, "Tom I love you very much and I love Anne." That made my whole day.

CHAPTER 12

HUMOR MAKES THE WORLD GO AROUND

There have been times while working in the group homes that I have felt stress or some sadness about a situation or a resident. Looking back over the fourteen plus years, I realized the good times far outweighed the bad. Humor was a release for all of us. Here are some of those moments.

John is a quiet spoken and kind person. One Sunday morning at Sunday school we were sitting and waiting for the class to start. The ladies from the Kelly Group Home came in with recently hired staff. In a few minutes John jumped up and went to the second row of seats and sat by the new female staff. I asked him why he moved. He said in all seriousness, "I am a gentleman and I need to sit beside this lady." John becomes infatuated with female staff from time to time, but is always truly a gentleman.

We were having dinner at the Cates home, and Peter, as usual, ate all of one thing on his plate before he went to the next item. We were not aware of any foods he did not like, and Anne had made creamed cauliflower. Peter, who is deaf and does not speak, put the cauliflower on his fork and started to put it in his mouth. He made a hissing sound like a cat. He went on and finished eating all of it. We wondered if he thought he was going to be eating mashed potatoes. It was a sound we had never heard.

Another evening Anne had fixed sweet potato casserole sprinkled with crushed pecans. It was delicious. I looked over and noticed that Peter was very carefully taking the pecans out of his mouth and putting them on the side of his plate. He thought they were seeds and didn't want to swallow them. I signed to him that it was okay to eat the pecans. He finished them all.

❧❧❧

Aalok is a high functioning individual, and one Saturday morning I was reminding him of his table manners. He was cutting up his pancakes and putting his sticky knife on the placemat rather than the edge of his plate. I discussed several things with him, then after breakfast we went into his room to see if it needed to be straightened. Noticing that the sheet was sticking out on the sides of his bed, I pulled the bedspread back and said, "Aalok, I see your problem. You have your top sheet running sideways."

His reply was, "Everything is my problem. That's why I live here."

❦❦❦

Marc was looking for his ski cap he would need for his snow skiing trip on the weekend. He could not find it anywhere and was getting a little upset. He told us that the "lady" had it. He had been skiing the week before in a Special Olympics event, and we assumed the lady was one of the chaperones that had been with him. We suggested he look in his room more thoroughly. A few minutes later I heard him talking in a loud voice in his room. I looked in and he was talking on a cell phone and he was telling the lady he wanted his hat. I finally realized that he was talking on the realistic toy cell phone his mom had given him. I think he found the cap, because if not, he would still be talking about it.

❦❦❦

A staff member at Matt's work place called me to say that Matt had gotten someone's thrown-away sandwich out of the trash can. They told him that he should not do that because of germs. His soft spoken reply was, "But I washed my hands."

One morning Anne went into Matt's room to wake him. It was not an easy task. Her usual method was to turn on the ceiling light in his eyes, pull the covers completely back and tell him he needed to get up. This particular morning Anne did all of these things. He smiled and said he would get up. Anne left and returned about ten minutes later to check on his progress. Matt had indeed gotten up, but only to shut the door, cut off the light, get back in bed, and pull the covers back up to his chin.

Matt enjoys eating and sometimes has a problem raiding the refrigerator or food cabinets after everyone has gone to bed. As a result cabinets are locked at bedtime and a web strap put around the refrigerator and tightened. He doesn't know how to release the strap from the refrigerator and doesn't know where the keys are to the cabinets. He does, however, know how to use scissors as staff discovered one morning when they saw that the refrigerator strap had been cut in half.

⁊⁊⁊

Barbara loves music. She can usually pick out and play familiar songs on the piano. One evening we had company for dinner and I asked her if she would play some tunes. She got up from the table, started over to the piano, and with a hearty laugh started singing, "There's No Business like Show Business."

Another evening at the dinner table Barbara announced that she was going to buy Rush Limbaugh's new book to give to her dad. Anne asked her what the book was about. Her immediate reply was, "Sex!"

I pulled up in the van with four of the ladies (including Barbara) and parked in the handicapped section in front of a local restaurant. Anne was coming in the car with two of the ladies to meet us there after they had run an errand. We got out of the van and waited on the sidewalk for the others. When Barbara saw them getting out of the car she said, "Look, here they come- act normal!"

One evening I was awakened by the door alarm going off at 3 a.m. I jumped up and ran into the kitchen. Barbara who had a restless night was taking the trash out to the cart by the back door. She had also set the table with eight placemats, silverware, napkins and cereal bowls for the next morning's breakfast.

On another one of her restless nights, I went to the refrigerator and found 24 cans of coke all lined up neatly on the front of three shelves. She had it all ready for a Coca Cola TV commercial.

Patty loves music, especially country. She tells everyone her favorite singer is Conway Twitty. She has also announced from time to time that she also likes, "that Englebird Hunkerdink man."

Rachel Ann loves keeping up with the Washington Redskins and Virginia Tech football season. She knows the time and dates the games are played. Being a graduate of Virginia Tech, I can always depend on her to give me the details on a Hokie game.

Rachel Ann also loves birthdays and is an expert on remembering dates including employees that no longer work at the group homes. Like many of the other residents, she enjoys making at least a week of celebration in honor of her birthday. She sends cards to staff and Sunday school teachers. I recall hearing about the time Rachel Ann sent a letter to one of her Sunday school teachers and said, "Next week is my birthday and most people give me money."

CHAPTER 13

KELLY AND CATES BELLRINGERS

Some years ago, we took the men from the Cates home to summer camp in New Castle, Virginia. One of the activities included the playing of color coded bells, accompanied by a taped recording of a song. The instructor used flash cards, and if you saw the color of your bell on the card you would ring it continuously. The instructor kept track of the beat by counting the numbers showing on the back of the cards. We played chords and harmony, instead of the melody, and I was impressed with the sound. This patented method of color coded bell ringing was a great idea and I wondered if we could do it with the residents at the group homes.

In 2000 Anne and I decided to invest in the bells. I ordered the system which consisted of thirty-two bells, four sets of flash cards and cassette tapes. We liked working with the residents, and they enjoyed learning to play. We practiced in Special Friends Sunday school class.

Marian Wiltshire, one of our dedicated teachers, heard us and had a suggestion. She was coordinating a Retired Teachers Association luncheon, and asked us to come and present a program. We decided to call ourselves the Kelly and Cates Bellringers, named after our two group homes. We accepted the invitation and were treated to a nice lunch. We then talked about how our homes had come into being, and the birth of the Bellringers. We played six or seven songs and enjoyed their applause and warm reception. Before we left several folks came up to us and asked if we could perform at their church. We ended up with four "bookings." Look out show business, here we come!

We performed at churches and civic groups in Maryland, Virginia, and North Carolina. Each year we did as many as ten to fifteen engagements. Over the years we increased our repertoire and now have over forty songs that we can play consisting of religious, patriotic, Christmas, and show tunes.

Churches have been very receptive to our musical programs and a number of them have invited us to perform more than once. We tell them about the miracle that took place in our Church that made it possible for us to have two beautiful Christian homes. Many times folks come up to us with tears in their eyes, telling us how much they appreciated our program. They are impressed that our group can make beautiful music.

Because we took our group home folks on annual vacations to Nags Head, North Carolina, I started trying to make contacts at some of the Baptist churches there. A former couple from Fredericksburg Baptist Church, Dennis and Jerri O'Shell, lived in Nags Head. I met them and arranged to have us play in their First Baptist Church of Kitty Hawk. When we came back the next year we again played at their church. They gave us the name of the pastor at Nags Head Baptist where we did a performance on the following Wednesday night. We received a good reception from both churches. Folks came up to us, visibly moved, and thanked us for sharing our talent with them.

One year while Anne and I were enjoying our personal vacation at Nags Head, I went to nearby Manteo Baptist Church and talked with the church secretary and left a video tape and a brochure. At the end of my two week vacation I checked with the church, and they said they would like us to perform in October when the residents of the group homes would be there on vacation.

On a Sunday evening at 6:00 P.M we arrived in their sanctuary. There were about thirty enthusiastic people in the audience. After the group played a few songs, I went into the audience and gave out eight bells not being used, and invited these folks to the front of the church.

They joined us in playing several songs and it was a fun evening. At the end of the service they decided to take up a love offering, though I always tell churches and other groups that we do not charge for performing. It is our way of giving back to the community.

After the concert they treated us to sodas and snacks in the fellowship hall and everyone was very friendly. The treasurer of the church brought me a check for $540. The deacon, Dick Flowers, who had coordinated our appearance said: "When our people are moved by what they see and hear, they dig deep into their pockets."

When we first started performing at churches, our uniform consisted of a white polo shirt, navy blue vests and beige pants for all. As time went on we accumulated monies through contributions and church love offerings, and upgraded our uniforms. Today along with the beige pants the men have white dress shirts and navy blue wool blazers with brass buttons. The ladies are matching with wool jumpers and white blouses. We had a special logo designed with two gold bells and the words Kelly and Cates Bellringers embroidered and sewn on the uniforms. As soon as we got the new uniforms we naturally started sounding better.

In one country church, a gentlemen came up to us after the service and said, "I just told the Minister that I have been coming to this church for fifteen years and this is the most meaningful church service I have ever attended". This made us feel very good. After every appearance we have made, people come up to me and the other staff and residents, and tell us how much they appreciate us.

Some statements made in other churches have been, "Who is that gentlemen ringing the bell with a smile on his face all the time? I felt like I was looking into the face of Jesus." A couple came up to me and said, "When you were playing Amazing Grace the sound of the bells was surreal. There were angels in this auditorium!"

In still another church a lady came up after the service with tears and said, "I want to hug that young man. He looks just like my son." She pointed to one of our young men who has Down syndrome. He had a wonderful smile on his face, was pleased with the attention he was receiving, and gave her a bear hug.

In my sister's church, in Upper Marlboro, Maryland, we received a standing ovation after our performance. The Minister of Music wrote me several weeks later thanking me for our performance. He said, "We know that our congregation enjoyed your program, because they don't often give standing ovations."

Traveler's Rest Baptist Church near Fredericksburg has invited us numerous times to perform. We have done several Sunday morning programs and the some were for their "Over 55" social group. They always treat us to a covered dish dinner before we play.

The staff, and especially the residents, enjoy the socialization that we are afforded when we make appearances. It gives us a chance to strengthen the resident's social skills, and for more people in the community to know that these are loving and caring people. Some churches and organizations allow us to perform for a total of forty minutes. We then play a half dozen songs, tell the audience about the miracle of the Group Homes, and allow the residents and staff to stand up, take the microphone, and introduce themselves. Audiences are moved and realize these folks are neat people. They enjoy the love and sense of humor shown by our residents.

One of our former staff, Boyd Cobb, had arranged for us to appear at his sister's church, Salem Baptist Church in Crozier, Virginia. They gave us a warm welcome. We performed at the early and the regularly scheduled services. They then treated us all to lunch at a cafeteria. Several weeks later they sent me a love offering check for $500.

Two years later we were invited back to the same church in November and played at both services. We also performed one evening in December for their Bethlehem Walk. The church congregation worked very hard to set up a little village like Bethlehem, where you were guided through to experience the place where Jesus was born. It was very popular and thousands of people went through it, at no charge. We played a thirty minute program for them under a very large tent, where a thousand people sat as they waited to be escorted through the Walk. This was by far the largest captive audience we had ever played. Some folks in the crowd stood up and applauded us.

When we had performed for them in November, they had again taken up a love offering. I did not hear from them for about three months. I was certainly not going to ask them about our money. In February I received a thank you note from them with a check. I had to pick myself up from the floor. We received a check for $1760! I wrote them a thank you note and told them the money would be used for maintaining the bellringer uniforms and for group home vacations.

The experience we had in one small country church will always stand out in my mind. After we had presented our program and just before the last prayer, the pastor asked all of the bellringers to come down out of the choir loft and stand at the front of the church. Practically the whole congregation came forward and personally shook hands and congratulated each of us. Our bellringers beamed with all of the attention they were receiving. We were like "regular" people.

In another small church the pastor came up to the

choir loft and personally shook hands with all of the participants. So many of the pastors are moved by our performance and it is reflected in the final comments they make. They point out that our folks, with their capabilities, use their talents to bring beautiful music to the world, and members of the congregation need to use their particular talents. That's a nice way of saying they should get up off their bottoms and do something for the church or community.

In 2005 I asked my Minister of Music, Mike Patch, to adapt a song for the Bellringers to use as our official theme song. The words of the song were so meaningful to our mission. I believed the song had been written for us. The song is "Somewhere," from the musical West Side Story. Listen:

> There's a place for us
> Somewhere a place for us
> Hold my hand and we're half way there
> Hold my hand and I'll take you there.

Mike arranged the music in the key of C, as were all the songs we play. Our eight different colored bells do not include sharps or flats. Mike also created the color coded flash cards that tells us who should play and when. He then contacted the publisher and requested permission to record "our song". When he explained who we were, some organization there agreed to pay the publisher the $300 fee for the rights.

I was invited to the Church the day the recording was to be made. Mike had set up microphones near the large pipe organ speakers. Susan and Josh Cruse were the sound engineers. Our Church organist, Shirley Onderdonk and Mike playing the piano, accompanied our Pastor Emeritus Howard Cates as he sang the words in his beautiful bass voice. Everyone did a great job. It is a wonderful recording.

When we play this song with the bellringers, our group home resident Marrs also sings the words. There are many times we get sustained applause and a number of times that we receive a standing ovation.

When that happens, I usually thank the audience and tell them about the time that Marrs (blind since birth) sang "The Lord's Prayer" at a Baptist Association meeting. On this particularly evening Mike Patch accompanied him on the piano. After he finished singing, I carefully led him down from the podium back to his seat. I told him that he had received a standing ovation. When we were coming home in the car that evening Marrs asked me, "Tom, what is a standing ovation?"

I read these lyrics of "Somewhere" to the audience before we play the song. I suggest that the words "Hold my hand and we're halfway there" is the hand of Fredericksburg Baptist Church and it members building the group homes. "Hold my hand and I'll take you there" is the hand of Virginia Baptist Children's home with their

DDM (Developmental Disability Ministry) agreeing to run the program. These two organizations are responsible for the creation of two beautiful, quality group homes in Fredericksburg. **There is a place for us** at 2508 and 2510 Salem Church Road. Even more important, there is a place for us in this community and world that loves us.

Even now that Anne and I are retired from the Group Homes, we are active with the Kelly and Cates Bellringers. For the last several years we have been very fortunate in having a member of our church, Becky Bennett, volunteer to accompany us on the piano for all of our engagements. This improves the quality of our presentation because the live music is so much better than taped. She interprets for the deaf in our church and does a special presentation with us by simultaneously singing and signing a Christian song during our church performances.

Tom and Joyce Mulcahy, retired Group Home Managers like us, continue to be a part of the Bellringers. They are very dedicated to this ministry and a tremendous help to us. Tom has a beautiful tenor voice and sings a patriotic song at the beginning of all our programs.

For me personally, the Kelly and Cates Bellringers have brought happiness and a sense of accomplishment. Our residents are meeting new people every day. The community is learning that this is a unique and loving population that has much to give. We are not taking from the community but are giving back. I want everyone to know about our folks and how much they have meant to Anne and me. We have twelve beautiful friends, who just happen to be mentally disabled.

The Kelly and Cates Bellringers

CHAPTER 14

A FAMILY BONDED

They grew up in Charlottesville, Virginia and met their freshman year in high school, where they were both cast in a school play. He escorted her to the school bus one afternoon and she was immediately smitten. He was outgoing, had a wonderful sense of humor, and his down to earth demeanor made him popular with everyone. She on the other hand was shy and studious. In time this would change.

Ken and Vivian had a beautiful small wedding on August 20, 1960. They both worked various jobs. Ken then began his career in hotel management and the two of them became resident managers. Then their first child, David, was born.

They did not enjoy living and working long hours and getting up from dinner to wait on arriving customers. David, however, enjoyed living there. He took ice to customers and got tips. Repeat customers would sometimes bring him candy and toys.

While living and working at this motel, their second child Kathy was born. It had not been an easy pregnancy. Vivian became very ill. She was trying to do too much. She had been working one job, also helping Ken, and raising a son. She went to the doctor who prescribed two kinds of medicines. She was told she was burning the candle at both ends. She had to quit working- and that was good.

A short time later, Ken was sent to manage a motel in North Carolina. Vivian was not happy being away from all her family support with a newborn. Luckily, after a year they returned to Charlottesville and managed various motels for about ten years until they arrived in Fredericksburg.

At first the family was not aware that Kathy had any medical problems. But then Vivian noticed that Kathy had difficulty sitting up in bed by herself, and she was now ten months old. She compared Kathy's accomplishments with a neighbor's little baby, who seemed to progress faster than she.

One day she took Kathy to a downtown store to have her picture taken. She placed her hand under her dress to hold her up for the picture. The photographer asked her if she thought there was something wrong with her child. Vivian was outraged and couldn't get out of the store fast enough. She had a suspicion but didn't want to deal with it.

Kathy began to laugh and smile at ten months old, but couldn't sit or pull herself up. She started walking when she was two years and five days old. The family was desperate and looking for answers and direction. Vivian recalled being in the office of a pediatrician when Kathy was five years old yet not potty trained. After the examination she asked the doctor what she could do for her child.

The doctor said, "You are doing a good job with her, and keep up the good work."

Vivian discovered a pre-school program run by a parent group associated with ARC (formerly known as Association for Retarded Citizens). No government money was available, so it came from the parents. She did not know all about the program, and had little knowledge about mentally handicapped children. But that would change!

Vivian took a tour of a pre-school facility that was located in the basement of a private home and walked by mentally handicapped adults who wanted to shake her hand. She didn't understand what they were saying.

Vivian said, "They looked as though they had disabilities

and I had this little adorable five year old, long haired, blond cutie that would grow up and never look retarded. I couldn't get upstairs fast enough and out of that door. I didn't want anything to do with them. It took me a long time to realize that I didn't need to understand what they were saying. I just had to smile and shake their hand. That was all I needed to know about the mentally retarded. They didn't expect me to understand their language. They just wanted to be acknowledged and respected."

Vivian began serving on the Board of Directors of ARC and later became its president. She served on state committees which is where her education began.

Vivian said, "I was on the road fighting for people with mental retardation. That was the beginning for me!"

Because she was involved with the State ARC, she got to know the National Director in Richmond. The two of them were an asset to Fredericksburg, when members of our church were advocating the building of our group homes.

When Kathy was seven, a law was passed mandating special education in the schools. It was difficult to see her go from the safe world of pre-school into public schools. No school buses provided transportation for special needs students. Kathy and other kids were transported by a crowded taxi with no supervision.

Vivian explained, "The parents have to be a constant watchdog, advocate, bad guy etc. I always felt we had to raise our voices and complain. If I didn't do that, Kathy and her classmates would have been in very bad situations."

When Kathy entered first grade in Charlottesville, there was only one building in the entire school system that housed all mentally handicapped students. They were not mainstreamed. There was a stigma attached to going to that school. Some of the parents did not want to sign the necessary papers to have their child in Special Education classes. Children fell behind in their work and were not getting a good education.

The next year plans were made to mainstream these students into regular schools. A law was passed requiring them to be in the least restrictive environment. Vivian and Ken were happy that Kathy would be going to the same school they had attended.

Then Vivian learned Kathy and the other students would not be inside the school, but in a building behind the school. She was upset, so she and the Executive Director of ARC went to see the Superintendent of Schools.

Vivian told the Superintendent. "I pay taxes to support these schools and you are educating my son in a regular classroom, but you are not educating my daughter in the same manner. I won't have this! The children ended up <u>inside</u> that school."

When Ken's job bought him to Fredericksburg, they settled in Spotsylvania County. The family had to fight the same battle. Kathy was to be put in a trailer behind the school. More battles were waged which took a toll on the whole family.

Vivian thought, "So here is a parent who has the emotional trauma of having a child who is never going to go to a prom, never going to marry, and will never be able to write her name. There is a physical and financial drain in taking care of my daughter."

There were no Medicaid dollars available at that time. Vivian and Ken both had to work and needed a babysitter when Kathy was out of school. Babysitters for a mentally handicapped person were hard to find.

Vivian and Ken were able to find someone to care for their daughter during the day. Mrs. Beach ran a child care center and was willing to take her first special needs child. Vivian said, "I found an angel in Mrs. Beach in Ferry Farm Subdivision, where we lived. I was so blessed, because we had just moved to Fredericksburg and I had to go to work. God put this special woman in my path."

The people in the school systems tried to be advocates for these folks, but the parents are the real champions.

"I was not born to be a fighter," Vivian said. "I was a very passive person. I hated conflict or argument. I was shocked to find out that I was a tiger. I was fierce!"

Vivian and Ken continued looking for answers. They heard of a program at a clinic in Pennsylvania known as the Doman Delacato Rehabilitation Program. It involved "patterning" exercises. At one point they had seventy volunteers coming in the home and doing pattern movements with Kathy six days a week, moving her arms and legs.

Vivian and Ken felt the doctors were egotistical and secretive about their methods. They spent several hundred dollars for Kathy to be tested. The doctor wanted to put her in the hospital to do exploratory work. The family would not be allowed to stay with her, but would be in a boarding house across the street.

They met anxious parents of children having brain surgery, possibly lobotomies. Vivian said, "I saw kids who looked like wet dishrags."

It was the worst of times for the family. They would not consider brain surgery nor would they leave Kathy alone in the hospital. They came home. The only good thing to come out of this experience was that with the patterning program, they were able to spend quality time with Kathy. The family was able to teach her a number of things that she formerly couldn't do. They began to learn more about the brain and mental retardation.

"The experience did not turn her around," Vivian said. "It did not make her normal. It is something I would never do again or recommend to other parents."

Vivian shared with me some of the emotions she and Ken experienced once they realized that Kathy was not going to be normal. They did not discuss it at first with the grandparents. Vivian felt the doctor secretly shared with the grandparents that this child might have medical problems.

Vivian said, "You want to protect the grandparents because this is their grandchild. They were smart enough to let this dawn on me in time. We were protecting each other. I don't know that it created a strain between Ken and me, because for one thing he worked all of the time which might have been a help to him. However, we were very bonded in our marriage, and we just wanted the best for Kathy."

There came a time when a grandchild, Sara, came into the West household as their son, David, was having some marriage difficulties. Vivian and Ken became the primary caregivers for her. This created additional stress on the family with Kathy exhibiting behaviors such as biting herself or tearing her clothing.

In time Vivian and Ken, with input from Kathy's case manager, made a difficult decision to have Kathy live for a while in the Central Virginia State Hospital in Lynchburg. I believe that her care there was good. From time to time Anne and I visited her and were authorized to take her out to walk in the mall and have lunch. We also accompanied Ken and Vivian on several visits. It was heartbreaking to see them take her back after each visit and hear the large steel door, with the small glass opening, slam shut as we walked down the steps and out of the building.

Some years later Ken and Vivian brought Kathy back to Fredericksburg. For a while she lived in a group home run by the Community Service Board in Fredericksburg. Later she was able to return home and live with her mom and dad.

On Sundays Anne and I would take Kathy after church to relieve her parents for the day, as we went to our gift shop to restock and do paper work. The store was closed. She would have lunch with us, and drink tea while sitting in a wooden rocking chair. We had old large FTD florist books that were to be thrown away. Kathy would spend hours tearing the pages one at a time and neatly putting the pages in the trash can. She was very content and we felt comfortable being around her. Her vocabulary was limited but she did learn to say the name of our shop, "Wee Wreath."

Kathy thrived living at home and had caregivers during the day while Ken and Vivian worked. Unfortunately, she developed some health problems and spent a time in the hospital two years in a row. Her heart was weakened each time. It was difficult to visit with the family in the hospital and see the sadness in their eyes. During the second hospital visit Kathy passed away on November 28, 2003 at the age of thirty-seven.

Ken and Vivian asked Anne and me, among others, to say something about Kathy's life at the funeral. One of the things we mentioned was that the family had provided a loving environment for their daughter and given her a good quality of life. It was a very sad day for all of us.

Ken and Vivian continue to heal and have a strong bonded marriage. They remain our very close friends.

As Anne and I look back on Kathy's short life, we came to realize how she influenced our personal life and became responsible for the creation of our Special Friends Class ministry where she became our very first student.

God works through many people to accomplish His goals and sometimes we just have to be still and listen.

And God said: *Kathy, you have done your work on earth. Come be with Me by My side in Heaven.*

CHAPTER 15

THE BENEFACTOR

The Mullins family graciously gave two properties, one with a ranch style home on it, to Fredericksburg Baptist Church to be used for our two group homes. John Mullins is well thought of in the Fredericksburg community. He and his family are owners of Covenant Funeral Service with several locations in the area. I have had several family members and a score of friends that have made use of their funeral services.

John had not always lived in Fredericksburg. I found it very interesting to learn why he had moved here. He consented to an interview during which time I realized why he has the reputation for being a kind and giving person.

John came from humble beginnings. He was born in a small town called Plankwood, located in the far southwest part of Virginia near the Kentucky border. He was the seventh of nine children. His dad was a coalminer and his mom a homemaker. She enjoyed cooking three hot meals a day. John and his siblings sometimes enjoyed coming home from school for a hot lunch. Most of the time, however, he took his lunch.

He graduated from high school in 1957. He had in his earlier school years been responsible for starting up the old potbellied stoves in a three room schoolhouse before the rest of the students got there. He remembered as a kid that he would bring biscuits with ham to school for his lunch and see other kids have white Wonder Bread for their sandwiches. He thought these kids must have come from wealthy families. He estimated that his family produced at least 90% of the food they consumed.

His mom always provided for the family with wholesome food, clothing, and clean beds. She canned up to 700 half-gallons of vegetables each year along with tomato juice and pickles. He helped by plowing the gardens with a five footed plow drawn by a team of horses. When the plow broke his high school shop experiences enabled him to fix it.

John, when fifteen, started working for a local funeral home under the DEO program that allowed him to receive work experience at a trade and continue schooling. The owner, thinking of the job experience as compensation, was somewhat thrifty and did not pay him for the first six months. John's dad wanted him to just come home and work on the farm, but John was determined to stick it out. John said, "When I got that first five dollars, I was very proud, and went up to the local restaurant and bought hamburgers, French fries, and a coke. I think it cost a dollar, and I want to tell you that was a good day."

After graduating from high school, John went to Arlington, Virginia to serve his apprenticeship. After graduating from there he married his childhood sweetheart Barbara. They had gone to the same high school. While in Arlington he worked two jobs and Barbara worked also. They saved $5500 to enable him to go to Mortuary school in Cincinnati. Barbara didn't work after they had their first child, David. John borrowed $500 from his dad in order to complete school. He was pleased to pay that back later. However he had no money when he had finished. He had taken the state funeral director boards while in school and took the state Embalmers Boards after finishing school.

He and Barbara started their own funeral home business when he was twenty-one. That funeral home is still in business. It was in the mountain area and they did around seventy funerals a year. The business would not be able to support their family, so he made several moves and managed other funeral homes. They continued to open other larger funeral homes in Virginia.

One day one of his employees came to Fredericksburg to pick up a body and transport it back to Wytheville,

Virginia. He was told that the funeral home was for sale. John said, "That's how we got here."

He bought Wilson-Smith Funeral Home about a year before his mother passed away. He and his wife Barbara took care of her in a small cottage behind the funeral home in Wytheville. She suffered from Alzheimer's.

His mom had not been in favor of him moving from Wytheville. However he said that he and his family could not have been any better received and treated than in the community of Fredericksburg. "We were grateful to have earned their trust. Without trust you don't have anything.".

I had not realized that John had operated that many funeral homes before coming to Fredericksburg. He said he used them as stepping stones to make a living, as his family was expanding. He said, "We were able to educate our three children." I was truly blessed and wanted to lay a foundation for the grandchildren. I give much credit to my wife Barbara, who is a helpmate, and has supported me in all of my endeavors."

The first time John met Herbie Embrey was at Fredericksburg Baptist Church. John was conducting a funeral there and was introduced to Herbie. He recalled that he was dressed in a shirt and tie and Jaycee medals all over his jacket. He knew that he was a person with special needs, but an exceptional individual. He was impressed that he spoke to him by name, whenever they met. He learned more about Herbie through the local Jaycees. The Jaycees were kind to Herbie and let him hold an "office" in the organization for many years. They loved him and he enjoyed all the friends he had there. Today the Jaycees honor him annually by awarding a Herbie Embrey Community Spirit Award to someone in the community.

John became aware of some of Herbie's living conditions. Herbie was very social and everyone assumed he could take care of his needs. We all learned otherwise. Consequently, when Fredericksburg Baptist Church was starting their efforts to create a group home for some of the folks in Special Friends Sunday school class, John and Barbara Mullins offered land for the building of the Mary Kelly Home. A few months later they gave adjacent property with a ranch style home to the church which became the Cates Home. This was done with the stipulation that Herbie would have a place to live for the rest of his life. Pastor Larry Haun made that happen. The Howard Cates Group home opened approximately a year after the Mary Kelly Home.

John said, "I was always proud that we knew where Herbie was and knew that he was eating well."

Everyone was shocked when Herbie passed away several years later. He was found in his bed after having died of a heart attack during the night.

The Covenant Funeral Home provided a wonderful funeral service and later installed a monument at the grave site. John said, "He was one of those people who may have had an impediment, but he commanded your respect as judged by the size of the funeral he had. He, as far as I am concerned, made our life richer as individuals. I am very grateful that we crossed paths in life."

John took a personal interest in Herbie over the years. New clothing was purchased for him. He was invited for visits and meals in the home. John, and employees of the funeral home, provided taxi service for Herbie to get to and from work. There were many friends in the community who also provided him with transportation.

During the interview, I thanked John for his generosity to the church and community. His modest reply was, "Herbie never made us feel uncomfortable. I am probably a strange duck to some folks but I was more comfortable in Herbie Embrey's midst, than I am in the richest environment. He was for real. He used what little he had to the best of his ability. That's my experience with Herbie. Thank you for taking care of him."

And God Said: *John, your loving heart and generosities have touched many. Be assured that your friend, Herbie, is by my side.*

CHAPTER 16

HERBIE

In 1965 Fredericksburg Baptist Church established the Fredericksburg Baptist Activities Center on the lower end of downtown Fredericksburg. The Center was built in an area of affluent homes that bordered the Rappahannock River on Caroline Street. The Rev. Richard Johnson and his wife Dorothy were hired to run the program.

Our church felt this would meet the needs of folks living in the downtown area who were of modest means and who felt uncomfortable in a church as large as ours.

In 1987 a decision was made to close the mission because of increasing costs and a membership that was not growing. I remember sitting in a meeting where some of the members of that mission were in tears and felt deeply that it should not close. The church welcomed all of those members and gave them the opportunity to become a part of the home church. We began a bus ministry for those in the city to use to attend our church.

One of those moving from the mission to Fredericksburg Baptist Church was Herbie Embrey. He later had a profound effect on a new direction for our church.

Herbie was a special needs person but he wasn't convinced of that. I remember the first time he came into our Sunday school room. He had on a suit and tie. On the front of his jacket were dozens of Jaycee awards he had received over the years. To say that he was a social person did not even begin to describe his personality. He was hyper and oozed happiness. He had a terrific mind for remembering people's names. It was as though he had taken the Dale Carnegie course and used all the rules. If I was in the hallway outside of the Sunday school room with him when church members came in, he knew all of them. He knew their kids names and would ask relevant questions about their offspring. After talking with anyone he ended the conversation by saying, "Okay, all right!"

Those three words became his trademark. Then he would walk away with very quick and short steps like Charlie Chaplin, the Tramp. Herbie was possibly the same height as that character, but had a weight problem around his middle and carried it proudly by standing up very straight.

He worked as a busboy at Shoney's at Four Mile Fork in Fredericksburg and later at the chain's restaurant on Route 3. He cleared tables and washed dishes, the least favorite part of his job. What he enjoyed doing was speaking to every customer that came in, talking to their kids, and inviting all of them to come to *his* Fredericksburg Baptist Church. When a repeat customer came in, he knew them by name. If his friend John Mullins from Covenant Funeral Service came in, he introduced him to any of the other customers in the restaurant. Herbie also enjoyed, on occasion, getting in the Shoney Bear outfit and standing outside waving to the traffic going by.

He lived in a subsidized apartment complex on Bragg Road. His case manager helped him with his finances. He would call for a taxi and go to the local community service board taking all his bills and paychecks to her office. She would have him sign checks for his expenses and give him cash for small purchases. He did his own grocery shopping. Transportation was not a problem for him. However I was aware there were times he used a cab to go to and from the drug store just to buy a candy bar, chewing gum, or batteries for his TV remote, radio, and flashlights.

Our gift and florist shop was next door to the drug store. Quite often Herbie would come in and socialize with Anne and myself along with our employees. They took a liking to him and on occasion provided him a ride home to save taxi fare. Whenever he came in, he would ask if we could do the wedding flowers for him if he found a girlfriend. We assured him that we would.

He had a list of phone numbers of his many friends, including mine, and he would call if he needed transportation. He would always wait outside his apartment for his ride.

One afternoon Herbie came to our shop as Anne and I were getting ready to go to Hardees for dinner. We asked him if he would like to eat with us and we would drop him back home later. His excited reply was, "Okay- all right!"

After eating we drove into the parking lot of the apartment complex. It was just turning dark. Herbie asked if we could come in and look at a green ivy plant in his living room that he thought might be dying. Anne said she would be glad to look at it.

We walked up to the second floor. He opened his apartment door and turned on the living room light. What we witnessed was unbelievable. Hundreds of cockroaches were scampering around on the walls and floor! I mean hundreds! It was like a horror movie! Some of them were crawling around a picture of Jesus. I removed it from the wall and dozens of cockroaches nesting there took off wildly in all directions.

Here we are with a mildly retarded, social, outgoing, healthy young man with good eyesight, completely oblivious to the cockroach infestation. My thought was, "God, thank you for killing that ivy plant in the living room."

To be continued....

❧❧❧

The cockroach brigade arrived the very next evening. Anne, myself, and Sherry, one of our employees, came armed with mops, brooms, cleaners and roach spray to remedy the situation. We discovered other atrocious conditions. The refrigerator was empty except for a container that had cloudy water in it. In the kitchen cabinet were three open cereal boxes with cockroaches gaily crawling in and out for an unlimited feast.

I went into the utility room and found dozens of empty paper grocery bags, some of them precariously close to the gas pilot light for the hot water heater. It ended up being a two night operation to get the apartment in order. The only thing really organized in the apartment was his coffee table in the living room. He had fifty or sixty matchbox toys lined up in rows running the length of it.

Herbie was pleased to have us in his apartment but was not inclined to be a part of the work crew. He was busy on the phone going down his list planning his transportation needs for the next several days. He had phone numbers listed in a little black book. If someone was not available he would go to the next number. We knew he would be a good candidate for our soon to be opened group home.

He was totally involved with the Fredericksburg Jaycees and held an "office" in the organization and remained with them for many years. At that time everyone who was a member of the Jaycees and had reached age thirty-five, became an "Exhausted Rooster" and would graduate from the organization. That is, everyone but Herbie Embrey. Today the organization annually presents the Herbie Embrey Award to a citizen in the area who has made a significant contribution to the community.

He knew people in the local fire department and rescue squads. Sometimes they let him ride with them on calls. He loved bluegrass and country music and became friends with some bands in the area. He was a member of the Good Time Cloggers and went with them to perform. It seemed that he knew everyone in town and he was loved by them all.

When we approached Herbie about moving into the men's group home, he was not sold on the idea. He was afraid he would lose his community contacts. We assured him that he would still be able to do all of the things he wanted to do. We suggested to him that he come live in the Cates Group Home for a three month trial basis. John Mullins was encouraging him to make the change. (I feel that John Mullins' love for Herbie had much to do with the decision his family made to give the Fredericksburg Baptist Church the properties and home on Salem Church Road.) Herbie finally agreed and was one of the first residents to move into the group home.

Each individual living in the home had his own bedroom. Herbie had the largest one in the house and his own private bathroom. He had all new furniture including a king size bed. We made sure he left the cockroaches at the apartment. All that came with him were his matchbox toy trucks and a large box of varied size batteries.

It didn't take long for him to adjust and realize that he had not lost any of his freedom, or access to his friends. He was now receiving good nutritious food, clean clothing, and loving care, sans cockroaches. We also convinced him to only wear two Jaycee medals at any one time on his suit jacket when attending church or other functions.

He still maintained his private "taxi service" for his excursions. John Mullins and family were part of that phone list as well as Bill Young. Bill was president of Heartland Bank in Fredericksburg and many times picked Herbie up for work before going to his own job. Bill's wife, Nancy, also became a part of his world. Herbie would phone her several times a week to talk. If a thunder storm was predicted he would call her and tell her to unplug the TV.

He loved to go grocery shopping with Anne. When they were in the checkout line, Herbie would talk with the cashier, asking her name or learning it from her ID tag. Then in conversation he would use her name several times asking about her family etc. (Aha- That's what Dale Carnegie would do!)

On one of these excursions he told Anne he needed to buy some batteries. She reminded him of all the many size and type batteries in his box at home. She suggested they check it out when they got home. He had a special flash-light but did not have any nine volt batteries. Back to the drug store they went.

He continued to work at Shoney's but on occasion I would receive a phone call from his boss concerning his work production. They allowed me to work with Herbie in the dishwasher room. I tried to show him how he could do some things more efficiently and become less stressed. There were times he would be crying and I knew he was trying his best. However, he longed to be just a bus boy in the restaurant gathering up dishes and talking with all of the customers.

One time we had three staff members managing the two group homes because someone was on vacation. One of our staff became very sick and I had to rush her to the emergency room at Mary Washington Hospital. Anne was left to prepare everyone at both homes for bed and every ten minutes or so would go next door to the other group home checking on everyone. After getting the ladies settled in bed, she returned to the men's home. When she opened the door she saw Herbie. She asked where the others were. His reply was, "I got them to bed for you." He continued being helpful to staff around the group home.

Three years later in May of 1996, while Anne and I were enjoying a family vacation at Nags Head we received a shocking phone call from staff. Herbie had a heart attack during the night and died in Mary Washington Hospital. We were all in a state of shock as this was totally unexpected. We came back home two days early from vacation.

I was asked to be a pallbearer along with others in the community who had a close relationship with him. John Mullins provided the funeral services. At the viewing John asked the residents and staff of the two group homes to remain after everyone had left. As we sat reverently in the funeral chapel, we suddenly heard toe-tapping bluegrass music. Herbie had asked if John would sponsor a bluegrass hoedown at his farm sometime. This was the best that John could do.

Cars, fire engines, and rescue squad vehicles lined up for the procession to the grave site at Summerduck, Virginia. A mile long caravan was created. Covenant Funeral Service coordinated the largest funeral procession that anyone could recall taking place in Fredericksburg.

Pictures of the procession along Route 1 and 17, and the final ceremonies at the gravesite were pictured in *The Free Lance Star*. There were several letters to the editor and a two column editorial revealing just how much this individual was loved in the community. One quote from the editorial stated, "Two minutes spent with Herbie was enough to make anyone feel good. He was a fast-walking, quick-talking ambassador for the human spirit. Herbert Lee Embrey gave a great gift to people in this community. He brought out the best in them. Herbie was Okay and all right."

Our residents had all attended previous viewings and funerals of family members. With their strong and simplistic faith they had taken that in stride. The death of Herbie was a different thing. He was one of their own. For over a year, when they took turns saying grace, the residents would mention him.

I will never forget when the residents and staff visited his grave a year later. John Mullins had donated a large headstone that had a red colored fire engine inscribed. We took a bouquet of flowers and gave one flower to each resident. One by one they went up to the headstone, said something to Herbie aloud, and then placed the flower on the ground. Even Peter, who does not hear or talk, stood reverently for several moments before placing his flower with the others.

It was an "Okay-all right" day.

Herbie Embrey 'Okay, Alright!

CHAPTER 17

THE NIGHT WE MET JOHN DENVER

Annie Felder was a member of our Special Friends Sunday school class for several years before moving into the Mary Kelly Group Home. She graduated from James Monroe High School with a Special Education diploma. I was invited to her graduation party. I don't recall what gift I took, but I was immediately aware she had a "thing" for John Denver, the country ballad singer. Annie had received a number of gifts and one of them was his newest CD. She told me that she was in love with him and that he had written a song just for her entitled "Annie's Song." I think she really believed that he had.

She moved into the group home in June 1993 and John Denver memorabilia came with her, including more music and pictures. She had a TV set in her room and her mom always kept her aware of television programs featuring him. Over the years Annie accumulated many VCR tapes and later, DVD's

Three years after Annie moved into the group home her mom, Paula, asked Anne and me if we would take Annie to a John Denver concert in Washington D.C. She would cover all expenses. We were not scheduled to work that day, and we looked forward to going.

It was a cold December day. The concert was in Constitution Hall that evening at eight p.m. I was concerned about parking and wanted to get there before dark. We had some additional time on our hands. The Festival of Trees was close by on the Mall and we walked through and saw all the Christmas trees representing each of the fifty states. It was impressive, but the tour took some time as Annie was unable to walk very fast. We were all shivering from the cold.

We forgot about the cold temperature when we got into Constitution Hall and saw her idol performing. I noticed that she mouthed many of the words as he sang. This young lady was in seventh heaven. Anne and I were very impressed with the concert. We had to walk back to the car in freezing cold afterwards, but Annie excitedly talked about what she had just seen and heard.

Several years later John Denver returned to the DC area in June and gave a concert at Wolf Trap. Annie's mom asked us if she could purchase concert tickets for Anne and me and everyone at the ladies group home and take us to dinner. We readily accepted.

Annie was very excited that day. She wore a tee shirt that said, "#1 Fan of John Denver." We got on the group home van and headed for the big city. Annie's younger sister, Pauline, also came along with her camera. Annie definitely wanted to get some pictures. Paula had managed to get two backstage passes to visit him after the concert. The rest of us planned to wait outside. Paula said to us, "Come with me." We followed her to the door leading to backstage. An attendant at the door said that she only had two visitor's passes. Paula pointed out to him that there were six ladies and three staff who wanted to see John Denver. He said that he could not authorize it. She wanted to know who could make the decision to allow us in. He pointed to his supervisor standing beside a door located further up the long hall. She and Annie walked up to him and Paula explained how important this visit was, pointing to Annie and her #1 fan of John Denver tee shirt. It worked.

We were all ushered into a large room where several groups of people were shaking hands and getting autographs. We were thirty feet away from where John Denver was standing. People were in front of him and we could not see him very well. Then they left and it was our turn.

Barbara Wright, one of the other group home residents, suddenly realized that she was in the room with a star. She bolted away from us and ran toward him saying, "John Denver, I love your music!" She grabbed him with her arms and gave him a bear hug. He appeared a little off balance and shocked, but quickly regained his composure as he saw the rest of us walking toward him.

He hugged all of the ladies and had them pose so Pauline could take their picture. They were in such awe and kept staring at him. He was very patient and took the time to have them all turn around and smile at the camera.

I then walked up, shook his hand, and thanked him for a great concert and being so patient with our ladies. He had a strong handshake and looked me straight in the eyes. I am over six feet tall and seeing him on television from time to time had led me to believe that he was not a tall person. He was very personable and down to earth.

We discussed the concert and I told him how much I enjoyed the new piece he had written called, "Foxfire Suite" He thanked us for coming and said he hoped he would see us again.

That would not happen. We were all saddened when we learned of his untimely death. Paula called me and asked me to make sure Annie was okay with the bad news. Annie told everyone that he died in an airplane crash and was now in heaven. She, like the other ladies, had a simplistic and strong faith. Anne and I continue to learn from these friends.

All of the ladies at Mary Kelly Group Home have a framed picture in their room to remember that special concert evening. We were all on a "Rocky Mountain High."

The Night We Met John Denver

CHAPTER 18

THE POWER OF A SMILE: THE POWER OF LOVE

His mom was a deaf mute. He was her seventh child and she abandoned him at the hospital in a small town in Pennsylvania. He would never know his father, his mother, or his siblings.

During the first six years of his life he was sent to three different foster homes. He was considered a problem child. During the first three years of his life he had not been potty trained. Staff from the foster homes documented that he could not talk.

He was sent to a Lutheran residential facility and was placed in the most profound and severely retarded unit. He did not see or hear well. Some of the staff there reported, however, they had heard him say a few words.

He was a handsome kid with a beautiful smile, blonde

hair and blue eyes. He did not look retarded. He craved attention and his smile was his way of getting it.

His name was Marc.

❧❧❧

She grew up on a small farm in Scottsville Virginia, the home town of John (Boy) Walton. She went to Mary Washington College and while there she and some of her classmates attended Fredericksburg Baptist Church pastored by Howard Cates. She had a calling for the mission field and wanted to be a nurse and received her RN degree from Virginia Baptist Hospital in Lynchburg, Virginia. She went to Africa and worked in Tanzania for four years in a tuberculosis hospital before returning to the United States.

She attended the University of Pennsylvania and while there received her master's degree in pediatric nursing. She taught for fifteen years. During a summer break from teaching she applied for and got a summer job as a nurse in a camp run by the Lutheran Home for mentally handicapped youngsters.

Her name was Joan Collins (not the actress, but a genuine star in my book.)

One of her jobs at the camp was to administer medications to the children while they were eating in the dining hall.

She said that her boss on the first day told her to carry the medicine in her hand and put it directly into the child's mouth. Joan would soon come up with a more sanitary method

All of that week she administered medications to the kids in the dining hall and noticed that one little boy at the end of a table watched her every move. On the third day she went to the office of the social worker and asked, "Who is that cute little blond headed kid at the table who keeps looking at me and smiling?" "That cute little blond headed kid?" repeated the social worker, and she paused. She then began to tell Joan about the little boy's problems including his going in and out of several foster homes, that he was a behavior problem, and did not speak. Joan found out that his name was Marc.

One week while participating in the camp, Marc was very sick with strep throat and stayed several days in the infirmary. As camp nurse, Joan was authorized to take him to her townhouse for the weekend to recover before returning him to camp on Monday. In the car he was very attentive and listened to the sound of the motor.

Joan had been told that he was on an adult dose of medication to get him to sleep at night. Staff had a hard time keeping him in bed. She said, "I took him upstairs and showed him the room he would use. He was now six years old. I think he would have sat in my lap the entire time we were there. I decided to put him in the bed and told him he needed to go to sleep. I sat at the foot of the stairs and only had to go back one time to tell him to go to sleep. I never had that problem again."

She took him back to camp and then started her month of vacation. After returning to work she asked to take him home for the weekend. They had his clothes packed in a paper bag. When he came into the townhouse he went into the kitchen and saw Joan's roommate and said, "Hi Pat," and then went upstairs to his room.
This was the first time that she had heard him utter words that could be understood. After knowing him for only six months, she considered adopting him.

She told me during the interview, "I was forty years old and not married. I did not have to worry about money to support him, but did have the concern as to who would take care of him while I was working. I thought everyone else does this and I can handle it. I also had the concern of how he would do after growing up, and when the time came that I was not around to care for him. After a lot of prayer, I thought it was the thing to do." However, Joan's mom and some of her friends were trying to talk her out of it.
Because she was unmarried and he an older child, a social worker came to the home and checked on them for a year while she was providing foster care. Joan took Marc with her to talk to a lawyer about adoption. She was embarrassed when Marc crawled under the table, but he tended to misbehave in public. She felt much of this was a result of being in several foster homes, and the

Lutheran home. She arranged for Marc to get glasses and a hearing aid. She recalled how excited he was the day they were driving home after getting his new glasses. He was sitting up in the seat and was looking all around. After he had gotten his hearing aid they attended the musical play, Gypsy, at Valley Forge Musical Theater. Marc was very attentive and hearing words and music with more clarity for the first time.

When she went back to sign some papers with the lawyer Marc was dressed in a suit. Later they were in the court and the lawyer presented the case. He said, "It would be hard for me to believe that this is the same boy Miss Collins brought into my office some months ago." The lawyer highly recommended the adoption. The judge said that he had been on the bench for twenty years and never approved a single person adopting a child.

Based on the lawyer's testimony the adoption was approved. It was 1972 and Marc was now eight years old. Each year Marc and his mom would celebrate his adoption date as well as his actual birthday.

Joan placed him in the local school system for hearing impaired and special needs people. He attended school there for about seven years and Joan was pleased with the results. When Marc was about nineteen Joan decided to move back to her home in Scottsville. Her dad had developed colon cancer and her mom needed her help.

She enrolled Marc in Albemarle County school system to complete two more years of high school. He adjusted well to the move and Joan was able to get a job at the Children's Rehabilitation Center. She held that job for seven years before transferring to the section that specialized in working with young children subject to seizure. She would remain there until retiring in 1996.

Marc got involved in Special Olympics and became a good swimmer and started learning snow skiing at Wintergreen Ski Resort. She took him several times during the winter months to work with an instructor that specialized in working with the handicapped. Marc enjoyed all of these activities and socialization, and made friends easily with his smile and easy going nature.

She met a lady from Fredericksburg who had a son also participating in Special Olympics. They were discussing their kids and plans they needed to make for their continuing care. Joan learned there was a Christian group home in Fredericksburg that had an opening.

She contacted Betty Burris, the Director of Baptist group homes in Virginia. Betty suggested that Marc come to their summer camp in Salem, Virginia to see if he was ready to leave home. Marc enjoyed the camp thoroughly.

During the interview Joan told me, "When I walked into the group home in Fredericksburg there was a picture of Rev. Howard Cates on the wall. I felt that was an omen. I knew him because I attended his church when I was going to Mary Washington College. I knew this was it."

Marc moved into the Howard Cates Group Home in 995. Joan said, "When I left Marc there, you folks suggested that I not see him for about two weeks. When I did visit I had a difficult time to convince him to go with me to McDonalds. He was afraid I wasn't going to bring him back. Because his room was a little small, I wanted to take some of his clothes back to Charlottesville. He would have none of that. He was very excited to be living there. As a parent it was reassuring that I made the right decision and that Marc considered this his home."

It was a pleasure having Marc there while Anne and I were supervisors. His beautiful smile, his willingness to perform chores around the house, made him liked by all. He continues to thrive in the group home and works in the laundry operation run by Goodwill Industries, and is proud of getting a paycheck. He enjoys visits with his mom from time to time and is still very active with Special Olympics.

We admire Joan's beautiful and selfless act as a single parent to adopt a special needs child and then allow him to move on. The power of a smile—it made a fantastic difference in the life of a young man named Marc Collins.

The Power of a Smile

CHAPTER 19

SAVING THE BEST FOR LAST

Working with Anne for twelve years as group home managers was a wonderful and fulfilling experience. This was my fourth career and the second job where the two of us worked together. I was fifty-eight years old when we first took the position.

This job was full time but I considered it part time work. We lived there for five consecutive days and then went home for five days. We alternated working shifts at each group home. A normal work day was around twelve hours and we worked an average of fifteen days a month. This work schedule was a great fringe benefit along with the health insurance and retirement benefits.

We considered the group homes to be our home while we were working, as we had our own private bedroom and bathroom. All of our meals and transportation were covered during this five day shift. When we took a five day vacation we ended up being off for fifteen consecutive days. This enabled us to take several mini vacations during the year.

Another realization was that our costs at home for food were cut in half. Our electric and water bills were reduced and home was close enough that we could always stop by and check the house and get our mail during the working shift.

Betty Burris, our supervisor worked out of her office in Salem, Virginia. We liked her policies and philosophy in running the group homes. Most of all she did not want to operate the homes like an institution. We were in accord as to what the homes should be and how we would manage them. She trusted us to make decisions, but we could call her anytime for advice. She encouraged us to have families involved and invite them to meals on occasion. When Betty visited us she usually spent the night, and many times we would be talking with her until midnight about the residents and families. We were all enthusiastic about being a part of a Christian group home. She genuinely loved the residents as did we.

We found it interesting and heartwarming when each resident first moved into the group home. Most of them knew each other because they were members of the same Sunday school class. Not a single one of them became homesick. However, some of the family members had to make some major adjustments. They had mixed emotions as to whether they were making the right decision for their son or daughter to leave the nest. We spent hours on the telephone with some of the families to reassure them that they had made the right decision. Their fears dissipated in the first few months as they saw their loved one blossom in the new environment. Most of the residents had siblings who had already moved out of the family home. Now they were able to do the same thing.

One widowed mom was having real problems with the decision she made for her son, John. She developed hives and suffered for several months. John, on the other hand, made a remark about three weeks after he had moved into the Cates group home. As he leaned back in his dining room chair one evening he said, "I like living here!" We immediately called his mom to let her know she had made the right decision.

Sheree's parents were invited to have dinner with us at Mary Kelly group home, several weeks after the move. As we were eating, her mom remarked that they always fixed Sheree's lunch to take to work. Dad came around to Sheree's chair and began cutting up her meat. The red flags immediately went up. We said nothing to the parents, but we knew what the first two goals for Sheree were going to be. Today, she cuts up any food on her plate and makes her own lunch. If you did it for her she would be very upset. These were small but good things that gave our residents more independence.

We considered ourselves each of the resident's extended family. We supervised them but it really meant caring for them in a loving family way. We provided transportation for them to go to work or to doctor's appointment. Some of the residents assisted us with grocery shopping and preparing meals. After the meals one resident was in charge of helping clean the kitchen and dining room. The residents assisted in weekly housecleaning and were responsible for keeping their own rooms clean. Some needed more help from us than others.

As in any other home with family members, not everything ran smoothly. We learned quickly that each resident was different and their needs varied. Sometimes a resident would have a behavior that could upset the household. Experience helped us to avoid many behaviors by learning what buttons not to push. The residents were adults but sometimes exhibited childlike behaviors. Having been parents made our job easier.

The residents went bowling every Tuesday after work. They attended Sunday school and church services weekly, as well as Wednesday night dinner and prayer meeting. We went to the movies on Saturdays and picnicked at one of the parks in good weather. They enjoyed shopping for new clothes. We went to concerts and antique car shows. For a number of years we went to Graves Mountain Lodge in October for the country music festival.

We did things that any other family would do. A member

of our church, Ted Humphries, liked what we did and for several years, until he retired, gave us checks annually for three thousand dollars to be used for vacations. Additional dollars were made available when the Kelly and Cates Bellringers presented programs at churches and received love offerings. We were able to take first class vacations together.

Beach vacations were a favorite. I recall the first year we went to Nags Head for a week during the off season. Anne and I were working in an ocean front cottage with the six ladies. The first evening we sat at the dining room table and looked out to see the waves coming up on the shore. The bedrooms were on the upper level. The next morning when Sheree came down to the dining room she looked out the window and said, "Look they turned the water back on."

Another year we went to Myrtle Beach, South Carolina and stayed for five nights. We rented five condominiums that housed twenty- two residents and staff. On the first floor of the motel were an indoor heated swimming pool, three hot tubs, and a lazy river. The residents would get in an oversize inner tube and the force of the moving water carried them around and around. There was something to do for everyone.

We had good kitchen facilities but we had enough money to have most of our dinner meals out. The highlight was when we dined at the Japanese restaurant where the food was prepared at our table. The chef was friendly and entertaining.

The residents were also excited to see Ripley's Aquarium with the moving sidewalk that ran through the glass tunnel. We were able to observe many fish species all in one holding tank that completely consumed us. The residents reacted to large sharks coming right up beside them and passing by.

Everyone enjoyed going to the Legends Theater and seeing some of the star impersonators. After the show, I was allowed to use my video camera and have our residents pose with some of the stars. The theater personnel were very accommodating. Marrs, with his beautiful singing voice, stood beside Bing Crosby. One of the other male residents and I stood beside Marilyn Monroe for our video shot. Everyone wanted to stand by Elvis. John, who had many Elvis records and sang karaoke every night in his room, was very excited to be posing next to his idol. I asked John who he was standing beside. His answer was, "The King!"

~ ~ ~

We retired from the group homes in 2006. The church provided a retirement party for the two of us and we were eternally grateful for the gifts of love we received that day. Anne received a beautiful diamond necklace and I got a lap top computer and started writing this book. The most valuable gifts, however, were the church members and friends thanking us for our years of service to the program.

As I now enjoy my retirement years, I look back and I am grateful to God for allowing Anne and me to be a part of his plan. To have a need and to witness how God put people and things together to make this ministry happen was mind boggling.

I will not forget the evening that Barbara, while sitting on the couch with Leigh, asked how far it was from Richmond to Heaven. My answer would be, "Barbara, it is only a prayer away!"

THE
JOURNALS

THE JOURNALS

I have worked at two group homes for the Rappahannock Community Services Board, and at the Mary Kelly and Howard Cates Group homes owned by Fredericksburg Baptist Church. I have had many wonderful experiences and attended workshops and seminars. At one of these sessions I heard the speaker make a statement that I will never forget. He said that the #1 disability was not mental retardation but LONELINESS.

Working with our folks, I realize how true is this statement. Each needs a friend. I then began keeping journals on some of my experiences with friends who have touched my life. Here are some of them.

MARGARET DILLARD

I first met her at Carriage Hill Nursing Home. One of our Special Friends Sunday school staff, Margaret Ingram, had been told there was a person living there who might want to join us. Our class worked with special needs folks of all ages.

I went and met the nursing home director who introduced me to our potential new student. Margaret Dillard was a short, small framed, gray headed lady, probably in her sixties. She was sitting at the activity table with several other people using crayons to color a beautiful lady training two circus horses to stand on their hind legs. I noticed that she was very exacting in her coloring inside the lines, and that she used more than one color crayon. The director and I sat down at the table with her and asked her if she would like to come to Sunday school and church. She said in a loud voice "Yes!" It was then I realized she was hard of hearing. I told her that I would pick her up the next Sunday.

That Sunday came and I pulled up to the front of the nursing home in my small VW Diesel Rabbit and walked into the nurses' station. I spotted Margaret in a beautiful blue dress with a Bible tucked under her arm. With a smile on her face she said, "I wait for you!" We told the nurses goodbye and walked out to the car. I opened the door and Margaret sat down slowly in the front seat. She placed her knees together and carefully pushed the dress down well over the knees. I told her that she looked very nice. She beamed!

We came to Sunday school and she had no trouble fitting in with the rest of the folks. It didn't surprise me to see that she did the best coloring.

At ten minutes to eleven, I walked her up to the church entrance. We went up the steps, received our church bulletins and walked into the sanctuary. Margaret was in complete awe of the size of the Church. She said, "Lotta people in here!" Heads turned. I whispered to her that we needed to be quiet. We continued walking up the aisle to the front where Special Friends were sitting.

Margaret was well behaved and at first a little apprehensive. She held on to my hand and Margaret Ingram's, who was sitting on her other side. Our new student being a small person could not put her feet on the floor. After relaxing a little, while still holding our hands, she began to swing her legs back and forth. I was reminded of my children when they were small in church swinging their legs.

For three Sundays in a row, I picked her up. I especially remember the third Sunday when our lesson was about Daniel and the Lion's Den. We again went up to Church services and sat together. Halfway through the service a small elbow hit me firmly in the ribs. It was Margaret with a big smile on her face, and her large Bible opened up to the Book of Daniel. I was flabbergasted! I didn't know that she could read or knew that much about the Bible. Later I found out from her family that was all she talked about that week.

The following Thursday the social director at the nursing home called telling me that Margaret had died quietly in her sleep as a result of a heart attack. I felt very sad.

On Friday I went to the funeral home for her viewing and met her brother and other members of the family. I went up to the open casket to pay respect to that dear lady. She was dressed in the same blue dress I had seen when I picked her up on that first Sunday. In her hands was her bible-opened to the book of Daniel. The tears came.

Today, thanks to the social director, I have that piece of paper with the beautiful circus lady and horses-- all colored inside the lines.

Tommy Higgins 12/91

Margaret Dillard's Drawing – All Colored Inside the Lines

DANNY THE COWBOY

Danny has been in a wheelchair all his life as far as I know. His means of communication is tapping his right foot on the floor or making a single syllable sound. He does attempt to point to his picture/word board placed under his clear plastic tray, but this is difficult because his arms are atrophied and folded upward toward his shoulders. His body is small and unsteady. This does not keep him from being happy, smiling, and laughing most of the time.

I did one-on-one mentoring with him for a few years, working part time with the Community Service Board. We became buddies. Often I took him out of the group home and pushed him in his wheelchair around the subdivision to get some fresh air instead of sitting and watching TV. One Saturday morning we decided to go to a movie. I wheeled him into the theater, and asked him if he would like to sit in a regular seat. He made his single syllable sounds and was almost jumping out of the wheelchair. I picked him up and sat him in the seat, moved the wheelchair out of the way, and then sat down beside him.. He was in seventh heaven. We were just two regular dudes sitting together watching a Saturday morning flick.

There were times when I worked part-time and stayed overnight. I was responsible for six residents living in the group home. Most of them were independent as far as their hygiene was concerned. Staff would help Danny with bathing and putting on his pajamas at night.

It was not easy trying to get him dressed after he had his shower. He would sit in his wheelchair and I sat on the commode seat top that enabled me to be on a more even level with him. Putting on shirts was especially difficult when trying to get hands, arms, and elbows into the sleeves. As time went on I became more proficient in getting him dressed. However, it never failed that I didn't work up a sweat.

One particular evening while helping him get dressed he leaned over, smiled, and gave me a hug with his small rigid arms. That made it all worthwhile. This hug from a person who can't talk, had just communicated volumes to me! He was saying thank you for helping me. Thank you for caring that I am clean. Thank you for being my friend.

At night when I put Danny in bed, he lay very still in the fetal position. When I covered him up, I usually put a tape or CD on his radio to lull him to sleep. In the morning he got out of the bed and crawled around on his knees pulling out clothes he wanted to wear. His favorite clothing-- cowboy hat, cowboy shirt, and cowboy boots.

He also selected video tapes that he wanted to pack and take to his day program.

I have not worked with Danny for over fifteen years, but see him on occasion at the Community Service Board day program where I am a board member. When I enter the room and he sees me, I hear noises made by his laughter and jumping up and down in the wheelchair. What a treat to see that big cowboy smile.

My wish is to be his friend forever. I know that he is mine.

THE MAN

A member of our Church called me and told me of a young person who had just moved into the 1208 House, an adult home on Sophia Street in downtown Fredericksburg, in which a number of our Sunday school members lived. Anne and I went there to meet Benny. He was a handsome young man in his late twenties. We talked with him and asked him if he would like to come to Sunday school with the rest of the class members who lived there. He communicated with us by nodding his head yes.

He took my hand and led us down to his bedroom. The room was very small and hot. On a small table by his bed were several small toy cars and trucks. He showed us his clothes hanging in the closet. We suggested the clothes that he could wear to Church. He again shook his head indicating that he understood. We told him that he would have fun and that the Church van would pick him up.

We said our goodbyes and started walking back down the long hallway toward the side entrance. I heard Benny say in a loud voice, "Hey!" We turned around and saw that he had stopped another resident in the hallway. He pointed to us, then to himself and said to the resident, "Mine!" Needless to say, we were hooked.

For a few years I was the number one person in Benny's life. Then "the Man," Hugh Mullen came along. Hugh, a longtime member of our church had participated in a number of foreign missions. Looking for a new challenge, he agreed to drive the van to Eagle Eyre in Lynchburg for the Mental Retardation Seminar Weekend that many of our folks enjoyed. While there, he and Benny became good friends. In Benny's room today you will find a framed picture of the two of them, arms around each other, sitting on a couch at Eagle Eyre.

Hugh is now one of our dedicated Sunday school teachers in the Special Friends Class at Fredericksburg Baptist Church. I truly believe that Benny was witnessing in his own way to Hugh. He and Benny sat together at Church. If Hugh was out sick or on vacation, Benny became very concerned and said, "The Man?"

I recently attended a board meeting of the Rappahannock Adult Activities Inc.(RAAI) where Benny is a daily attendee. A staff employee, not knowing that we were in the room, sent him in on an errand. There were fifteen people in the room and Benny, with a smile on his face, walked around the room stopping where I was seated. He playfully put his hands on my head and then put his arms around my shoulders. This made me realize that I still had a good friend and might be tied for number one spot with Hugh Mullen "the Man".

MIRACLE OF THE RED SUSPENDERS

One Sunday morning Hugh Mullen and I were helping class members get out of the Church van and walk into the Sunday school room. One of them, Tom, was a small man in his thirties who lived in a group home owned by the Community Service Board. He was usually happy and quiet. This particular morning he was upset about something. He communicated only by making a "zz" sound and reached for our hands to get attention. We could not understand what he wanted. He sat down at the table and it was apparent that he was not a happy camper.

Hugh noticed that Tom was not wearing suspenders, which was unusual. We had never seen him in church without them. As we were sitting at the table, more class members arrived. In a few minutes one of our teachers, Donna Updike came in and Hugh, jokingly, said to her, "Where are the suspenders?"

Donna looked surprised and said, "What did you say?"

Hugh pointed out that Tom was unhappy, possibly because he didn't have his suspenders.

Donna said, "Wait a minute" and walked out of the room. Hugh and I were even more puzzled.

A few minutes later, Donna came back into the room with a Christmas wrapped box. She gave it to Tom who immediately tore it open. Inside was a bright red set of suspenders! Tom was all smiles and we helped him put them on. Even now we don't know why Tom was upset that day. Whatever it was, the suspenders made him forget about it.

What makes this story very special is the fact that it took place on a Sunday in March, not December. Donna and her husband had kept the package in their car since Christmas and had tried each Sunday to give the suspenders as a joke to a church member who had never shown up.

I now realize only God could have arranged this wonderful sequence of events.

MIRACLE OF THE HEARING AID

I first met Pat in Special Friends Sunday School class. He was in his late thirties. He was profoundly deaf and did not speak. You could clap your hands loudly, standing close behind him and possibly get a response. He made sounds when you smiled or acknowledged him and had a good disposition. Pat had fallen between the cracks when he was growing up, as there was no special education in the school systems at that time. He probably will never reach his potential, but he appears happy in his world, and that is what is important.

Pat lived in an adult home with much older residents. The staff was not equipped to work with someone with mental disabilities. I learned the residents had a cold breakfast, a hot lunch, and dinner consisted of sandwiches. Normally that would be okay for most of the residents. However, because Pat went to a day program, he missed out on the hot meal. I agreed to become his legal guardian to remove him from this poor situation, and worked with the Community Services Board to get him into one of their group homes. This home provided twenty-four hour supervision for folks with mental disabilities.

Some years ago I volunteered to take Pat to an audiologist

in Richmond. His case manager had access to financing through a local civic club in Fredericksburg. Pat and I went into a small sound proof booth. He had on earphones and tried to respond to sounds by pointing his fingers up when he heard a sound. He managed to handle this for about 30 minutes before wanting to get out of the confining booth. Somewhere along the way no one followed through and Pat did not get a hearing aid until 3 years later.

I started working for the Community Services Board in the group home where he lived. Pat and I went for several appointments with an audiologist in Arlington, Virginia and I will never forget the final visit when he got his new hearing aid. The lady audiologist placed the hearing aid in his left ear. When she spoke to him he immediately responded by making sounds. The audiologist and I were overcome and embraced in tears of joy. We both realized that we were seeing a man in his forties, who until this very moment had probably never clearly heard the audible sound of a human voice!

As Pat and I were driving home on Interstate 95 that day, I sang songs like "Jesus Loves Me, and This Little Light of Mine". I was trying to sing on key while sitting beside me was this very bass voice, making off- key sounds, every time I uttered a word. Someone driving past and seeing us must have wondered what we were doing.

They were witnessing the miracle of the hearing aid.

THE SODA

It was our first full day at Nags Head and we were looking forward to our two week stay.

I walked along the water's edge, listening and watching the waves and the sea gulls above, feeling exhilarated. It was time for R and R away from the two group homes where Anne and I worked as Senior Residential Managers.
Returning to my beach towel, I lay down and listened to my Walkman hearing music by Michael Crawford, Barbara Streisand, and Frank Sinatra. Laying there I was determined to forget that it had been a hectic week, with one staff sick in the hospital, and two new staff members needing to be hired. We were here for two weeks and didn't need to think about staff or residents.

Looking at my watch, I decided two hours in the sun was enough for the first day. I walked back to the cottage, took a shower, dressed, and relaxed to the music coming from my recently purchased boom box with remote control.

I went to the refrigerator and pulled out a can of Coke Classic. As I relaxed and began drinking, I looked at the writing on the bright red can. It said, "1928-1996- 68 years of Olympic support." My mind wandered, started thinking of the men at the Cates Group Home who had recently participated in Special Olympic swimming. As I continued to sip my cold drink, one resident came to mind. Peter was a handsome young man, who was deaf and autistic. He worked at a sheltered workshop doing piece work. If he met his goal of so many units, his supervisor gave him money to buy a soda out of the machine at the end of the day. The incentive technique seemed like a small thing, but meant a great deal to him.

Like many folks with autism, Peter shows little response to hugs or touches. He averts looking directly at people and sometime will squint his eyes. Some time ago Anne and I and the five men from the group home went to a small circus sponsored by local Jaycees. We were sitting on the bleachers and I was off to one side observing Peter. His eyes were open wide and brightly showing excitement. He was laughing at a clown's antics and clapping his hands.

This made me realize that visual stimulation was very meaningful to him. I only wish I could share my love for hearing music with him. From time to time we had gone to local dances and let him put his hands on the loudspeaker. He seemed to enjoy the vibrations.

One night after he had worked all day and had earned

a soda, he went to the refrigerator, got his drink and prepared to open it. Anne wrote on a piece of paper, "Peter, can I have some of your soda?" She eased a glass over by his canned drink, and walked away from the kitchen counter. A moment later he was pouring more than half into her glass. This made me realize that, although he shows little emotion, he is a kindhearted and unselfish person. He had just given up much of his hard earned, special incentive pay. It was apparent that he had grown up in the arms of a kind, loving, and supportive family.

So much for my first day of vacation at the beach.

SUMMER CAMP

On a Monday morning in September two group home managers and I took our six men from the Cates group home to Camp Bethel, located in the western part of the state. The weather was nice with mild temperatures and a week of sunshine predicted. Our cabin housed all our campers plus two extra campers from the Richmond area to supervise for the week.

One of them was Bobby, a quiet guy with a nice smile. He did not speak but seemed to understand when we gave him directions. He was easy going and participated in many of the activities.

Bobby had a wetting problem, and unfortunately our cabin had no facilities. At least twice during the night I would wake him up and we would walk fifty yards to the bathhouse. During the day I would constantly remind him to use the bathroom.

Still, there were many wetting accidents which caused me to daily gather bed sheets and clothing and take them to the staff headquarters building to use the washer and dryer. I continued to stay on Bobby's case all week.

On Friday morning, after breakfast, we packed our campers and their belongings, for the trip back home. As I was getting ready to get in the van, I saw Bobby briskly walking over from his van to ours, and wondered why. I was pleasantly surprised when he smiled, extended his arms, and gave me a goodbye bear hug.

No words were spoken and I knew that all of the nighttime journeys to the bathhouse and trips to the laundry were worth the effort.

WHILE WALKING THROUGH THE PARK ONE DAY

One Sunday afternoon in May I took Pat, Benny, and Jeff to Alum Springs Park. It was a beautiful, warm and sunny day. We ate a picnic lunch and decided to take a little hike through the park for exercise.

After a short walk we came upon the crystal clear water making its way down the stream. I came up with the terrific idea of taking our shoes and socks off and wading into the water. I couldn't get any takers except Pat. While Benny and Jeff sat down by the stream, Pat and I made our way into the water. It was ice cold, and the rocks hurt our feet. We stayed for about two minutes! Pat and I helped each other back up to the bank where the others were sitting. We had mud and leaves all over our feet as we sat down.

I didn't have anything with which to wipe our feet. I decided I would take Pat's socks and try to wipe off his feet. What a mess! After I got him somewhat cleaned up, I got ready to clean off my feet with my socks. At that moment, Jeff who was sitting to the left of me said, "Wait Tom". He grabbed my left leg and bent my knee so that he could reach my foot. Without hesitation, he took his clean hands and began wiping the mud and leaves off of my foot.

I got cold chills as the story of Jesus washing the feet of his disciples rushed to my mind. I looked up, saw the gently swaying trees and blue sky, and silently thanked God for this very special moment with my friends in the park.

Jeff – The Foot Washer

BIOGRAPHY OF THOMAS J. HIGGINS

Tom Higgins was born and has lived in Fredericksburg, Virginia all of his life. He has a B.S. Degree in Business Administration from Virginia Tech.
He worked in personnel for the Department of Agriculture for seven years in Washington, D.C. He visited colleges in Virginia and Pennsylvania and recruited engineers, accountants, and administrative assistants.

He left that job and opened a gift and florist shop in Fredericksburg with his wife Anne. This business continued for twenty-five years. He and his wife then became supervisors for two group homes for the mentally handicapped owned by Fredericksburg Baptist Church. He and his wife retired in 2006 after working there for fourteen years.

Tom has been active for over twenty years as a teacher in a Sunday school class for the mentally handicapped at Fredericksburg Baptist Church and an active board member of a day program run by the local Community Services Board that serves many of the folks in the Sunday school class and others from the community.

He is a member of the Rappahannock Riverside Writers in Fredericksburg. He entered the work "Margaret Dillard" written in 1991, into the recently published Riverside Writers Anthology. This was his first effort in writing about his experiences in working with individuals with special needs. This work in 1995 was entered into the Church program on a Sunday morning at Fredericksburg Baptist Church that highlighted Mental Retardation Month. He received many positive comments. He then made a decision that he would do more writing when he retired.

Tom is working on his first book which is a biography that concentrates on the experiences he and his wife had in working with the mentally handicapped.

In 2010 he was recognized for his long term service by receiving two awards. The Fredericksburg Jaycees presented him with the Distinguished Service Award and the Rappahannock Community Services Board presented him with the 2010 Distinguished Intellectual Disability Volunteer Award.

The Author and his Wife